THE
Lost &
Found

THE
Lost & Found

Katrina Leno

HARPER TEEN
An Imprint of HarperCollinsPublishers

HarperTeen is an imprint of HarperCollins Publishers.

The Lost & Found

www.epicreads.com

ISBN 978-0-06-223120-8

Typography by Alison Klapthor
16 17 18 19 20   PC/RRDH   10 9 8 7 6 5 4 3 2 1
❖
First Edition

to my parents:
for everything,
ever

PART ONE

PART ONE

Lost

ONE
Frances

My grandparents' mailbox is shaped like a tiny replica of their house.

The bay window in the front, the glass-walled solarium on the side, the second-floor balcony off the master bedroom—everything is miniature and perfect and done in 1:12 scale.

My grandmother is strangely proud of this mailbox, probably because she paid a fortune to have it custom made fifteen years ago. I've seen her with a tiny can of paint and the most delicate paintbrush, repainting the shutters so they stay shiny and perfect. I've seen her pulling miniature leaves out of gutters the size of straws.

It was big and faintly ostentatious and kind of a work of art, in a weird way, and I'd been standing in front of it for five or six minutes, trying to get up the courage to open the tiny garage door, which is where the mail went.

I hadn't checked the mail in years.

The mailbox, while impressive, has always been a source of unlikely danger.

Just a few days after I moved into my grandparents' house on the Miles River in Maryland, my grandfather caught a black widow spider spinning a web in between a bill for my grandmother's subscription to *Good Housekeeping* and the morning paper.

He trapped the spider in a coffee canister and paraded it around the house loudly, making a big show of it. I asked to see it but was denied.

"Well then, why did you bring it in the house?" I asked.

"Just giving it a little taste of the good life before I set it free."

"Where are you going to set it free?" I pressed him. I extended one hand to touch the side of the coffee canister, and he swatted me away.

"Don't worry," he said. "Far away from here."

He set the canister down on the kitchen table while he got his coat on. I watched from the doorway.

"Are you sure I can't see it?" I asked.

"I'm sure," he said. "And you know what? You better not get the mail anymore, Frannie. These things are like pigeons. They can always find their way home."

I had no great desire to prove my bravery by risking a bite from a black widow spider, so I avoided the mailbox after that.

For five years I walked a wide, careful circle around it. For five years I checked underneath my pillow and in between my sheets for relatives of the black widow that had once famously moved into the nicest mailbox-house in Easton.

But as warnings often do, that one grew stale.

And after five years (and six minutes) spent gathering my courage, I opened the miniature garage door and withdrew the mail from inside.

The letter I was expecting hadn't come yet.

Bills, a flyer from our local grocery store, a few credit card companies begging for my grandparents' business. Nothing interesting.

I put everything back in the mailbox, but one letter slipped out and fell to the ground. It was addressed to Mr. and Mrs. Jameson, and when I picked it up I read the return address, stamped slightly crooked at the corner: the Easton Valley Rest and Recuperation Center for the Permanently Unwell.

But no—

Was one of my grandparents sick? Could they be keeping something like that from me?

I tore it open, terrified, and scanned it quickly.

It was a bill for a coffin.

I read it again, confused, slowly, trying to understand the words typed out in some small, precise font.

It was addressed to my grandparents.

My brain picked out bits and pieces, unable to process the whole thing at once.

> Dear Mr. and Mrs. Jameson,
> We have received your initial down payment.
> Coffin.
> Remaining balance.
> Our deepest sympathies.
> Please call if you would like to discuss payment plan options.

My grandparents had bought the coffin at a discounted rate. They had paid two hundred dollars of the fourteen hundred owed. It was originally two thousand.

It was a fourteen-hundred-dollar coffin.

For my mother.

But my mother had moved to Florida five years ago. My mother had taken the remainder of our money and left me to live with Grandpa Dick and Grandma Doris.

My mother wasn't dead. My mother hadn't died. And my mother had certainly never been at the Easton Valley Rest and Recuperation Center for the Permanently Unwell.

Unless . . .

Suddenly I wasn't so sure there had ever actually been a spider in our mailbox.

I don't have a lot of memories of my childhood.

My therapist said this was normal, probably some form of repression coupled with post-traumatic stress.

The first thing I can remember is an ice-cream cone.

My father bought me an ice-cream cone from an ice-cream truck. He handed me the cone, and I dropped it on the ground. I was maybe three or four. My canvas shoes had tiny giraffes printed on them, and the ice cream splattered on the toes.

He wouldn't buy me another cone.

I won't lie: I wish my first memory was a nicer one. I wish I remembered eating cake at my third birthday party or petting a dog for the first time or going to a park with my mom and being pushed a little too high on the swings.

But I guess we don't get to choose those kinds of things.

After the ice-cream cone incident, I remember some birthday parties, a first bike ride, some memorable Christmases, some blizzards, and some heat waves. But nothing really substantial sticks out until I was nine years old.

That is when my father either tried to kill me (if you listen to my mother) or just lost his temper but did NOT try to kill me (if you listen to my father).

• • •

What happened was my father and my mother had an argument.

The reason for the argument is not important. Who was right and who was wrong is not important. The beginning of the argument is not important.

The end of the argument is the important part, because that is when my parents wouldn't stop yelling and so I started yelling, at the top, top, top of my lungs until my voice cracked and my parents had to stop yelling at each other and start yelling at me, trying everything they could to shut me up until finally my father uncapped his fountain pen, strode across the living room, and stabbed me with his right hand. Just above and to the left of my belly button.

When my father let go of the pen, it stuck out of my stomach at a right angle. I was wearing a pink-and-white bikini. In another scenario, it would have been funny.

My mother screamed.

My father put his hands up like, *Oh shit, I fucked up,* and he backed away from me slowly.

I watched the blood leak out from around the pen, and the blood was almost black. Was it blood or ink? I couldn't tell which was which. It was all the same rich, thick darkness.

It leaked out of me in a thin river that filled my belly button and stained my bathing suit bottoms.

My mother screamed again and yanked the pen out of

my stomach (which you are not supposed to do, we later found out).

In the hospital after it happened, my mother held my hand before they wheeled me into surgery. I was crying and my stomach hurt and my clothes were ruined but my mother's face was incredibly calm, almost smug.

"You're gonna be okay, Heph," she said. She pronounced it like *Hef.* I generally discouraged the nickname, but I tolerated it then because I thought I might die in surgery and this would be the last time I ever saw her. And I didn't want the last time I ever saw her to be marred with an argument about my name.

Regarding my name, this is how I got it:

My mother requested the maximum dosage of painkillers and a birthing doctor who was notoriously lax with the meds.

She fell asleep halfway through a push. They had to wake her up and remind her where she was.

"I was having a really nice dream," she said.

"You're about to have a really nice baby," the doctor said.

"I want to call her Hephaestus," she announced.

"That's a terrible name," my father said. "I thought we were calling her Margaret."

"It was in my dream. Just now. It's Hephaestus or nothing."

"What kind of a name is that? It's a terrible name."

"I heard it somewhere," she said.

Hephaestus was the Greek god of metalworking. I'm not sure why it just suddenly occurred to her.

"We are not calling our baby Hephaestus," my father said.

"You have to push now," the doctor said. "I'm sorry to interrupt, but you have to push."

"I hate the name Margaret, and I hate you!" my mother said.

"Pushing now, naming later," the doctor said.

My mother pushed.

I slid out of my mother's body and into the doctor's waiting, bloody hands. He handed the scissors to my father and then looked at him expectantly.

"Hmm?" my father said.

The doctor looked from me to my umbilical cord and then back to my father again.

"Oh," my father said. "Okay. How important is it that I do it?"

The scissors were removed from my father's hands. A nurse cut my umbilical cord, the sacred rope that served as an in-between from the world inside to the world outside.

The tether that linked me to my mother. My mother who promptly fell asleep again as soon as I was free of her.

I know all of this is exactly how it happened because my father brought a video camera into the birthing room. He pressed Record and then left the camera on a table. The lens was pointed at my mother's vagina.

My father named me while my mother was sleeping. He had been prepared to call me Margaret but he settled for naming me after himself. Frances.

When my mother woke up, she threatened to put me back inside her if Hephaestus wasn't at least my middle name. She pointed out that was a perfectly fair compromise.

My father pointed out you couldn't actually put a baby back inside a womb, but he obliged her request.

It's nice to meet you.

I am:

Frances Hephaestus Jameson.

My mother got full custody in the divorce proceedings—I mean, duh, obviously—because my father was in jail serving a twelve-month sentence for stabbing me with a pen.

For a while it was great.

My mother and I were thick as thieves, united against this common enemy (my attacker!), spending the settlement money like it was a lot more than it actually was, buying new clothes and new shoes and growing our hair long enough to wear braids down to our butts (in her post-divorce state, my mother had reverted to her earlier hippie inclinations), and doing interviews for local news programs.

People were really interested in my story for a number of reasons, but probably mostly because my mother cried buckets of tears on camera while still managing to look completely flawless. Her mascara never ran. Her hair was always shiny. Her eyes were always bright. I think people were just truly interested in how she managed it.

My mother was present and invested in my life. She was a best friend, a comrade, a partner-in-crime. We traveled around the country together in one of those very old VW vans that always smelled faintly of dirt. I felt like I was really a part of something. We were a team, my mother and I.

Only she turned out to be just as crazy as my father. And then it wasn't so great.

Then one day I got off the school bus and it wasn't my mother waiting for me. Instead, my grandparents stood huddled underneath an umbrella (it wasn't raining, but Grandpa Dick opened an umbrella the moment the sky turned even the slightest bit gray).

"Oh, hi," I said.

"You tell her," Grandpa Dick said.

"Honey, we have something to tell you," Grandma Doris said.

"It's about your mother," Grandpa added.

"I thought you wanted me to tell her?"

"So tell her."

I waited. Grandpa Dick turned around. Grandma Doris put her hand on my cheek.

"Oh, Frances," she said. "We love you so much."

• • •

After my father stabbed me, after my mother pulled the fountain pen out of my stomach even though you are not supposed to do that, after I pressed my fingers into my stomach to try and stop the bleeding, after I asked everybody to please stop staring at me and call an ambulance, after the ambulance ride and the hospital and a couple surgeries and a ton of X-rays later, a doctor came into the room with a funny sort of smile on his face and said, "Okay. Here's the thing."

And that is how I found out that the nib of the fountain pen had broken off and stayed inside me, and this is the most interesting part of the whole thing, in my opinion: they never found it.

Now I set off metal detectors. They pat me down. They get the metal detecting wand and wave it over me.

Every time, it beeps in a different place.

Since then, I have always lost things. My grandparents called me forgetful, my aunt Florence called me absent-minded, my uncle Irvine said I was preoccupied.

But that wasn't it. I wasn't forgetful or absentminded or preoccupied.

I didn't lose things.

Things left me.

TWO
Louis

It was two forty-five in the morning, and I had just finished dusting our entire living room.

This wasn't that strange. I've never really been good at sleeping.

Even before the accident, I didn't sleep much.

My mother joked that we had gotten things mixed up in the womb. Willa could sleep twelve, thirteen hours at a time, easily, and I was up at one in the morning building Lego sets or finishing homework assignments or reading the Chronicles of Narnia for the fortieth time (in publishing order, sometimes, chronological order other times).

After the accident it got worse.

What had become normal sleeplessness for me was replaced by a frantic kind of awakeness, a state of constant consciousness. Now, instead of reading, I lay in bed and counted my breaths or went up to the roof and counted stars or went into the kitchen and counted jars of spices. Sometimes I did chores. Nothing too loud. No vacuuming or laundry. I loaded or unloaded the dishwasher, cleaned up the living room, took the recycling down to the lobby.

And because nobody in my family seemed to be able to remember that the mail comes six times a week, I checked our box in the lobby of the building.

Which is how, just before three in the morning, I opened a letter addressed to me from the University of Texas. I read it with the mailbox door still open, the other bills and flyers and coupons lying forgotten and unimportant, some spilling out to land on my feet and on the original tiled floor of the building that had been featured, once, in an issue of *Architecture Magazine*.

> *Delighted to inform you.*
> *Accepted.*
> *Full scholarship.*
> *Division I tennis.*

I put the letter into my back pocket and gathered up the rest of the mail.

I read the letter again in the elevator.

I read the letter again in the kitchen after dumping the rest of the mail into a basket my mother kept on the counter for just this purpose.

I read the letter again and again, making sure I was getting it right, making sure it actually said what I think it said.

I read it so many times that finally, for the first time in a week or two, I felt really, genuinely tired.

I fell asleep in an armchair in the living room, the acceptance letter taking up too much space in my back pocket, like it had somehow grown in size since I'd found it in the mailbox.

I woke up panicked from a dream about a helicopter.

I'd been hanging off a fire escape by just the tips of my fingers. A toy helicopter buzzed around my head and every few moments dive-bombed my hands, trying to dislodge my grip.

I had this dream a lot.

When I opened my eyes, Willa stood in front of me in the living room, a dish towel thrown over her shoulder. She cocked her head and stared at me, concerned.

"Are you okay?" she asked.

"Bad dream," I said.

"You were counting in your sleep."

"No I wasn't."

"Yes you were."

My childhood therapist had taught me to count through moments of anxiety. I guess the conditioning ran deep; I was doing it in my dreams.

"You're supposed to be helping me wash the dishes," she continued.

"Where is everybody? What time is it?"

"It's early. Like, too early to be awake in the summer, except Mom woke me up and told me I was wasting my life sleeping and if I didn't get up immediately she was going to send me to live with Auntie Anta until September. They're at the store, by the way. You're supposed to be helping me."

"I'll dry," I said, and stood up.

Willa stared at me. She wore some chambray dress (our parents own a fabric store, otherwise I would not know what chambray was) that stopped above her knees so you could only see her fake legs and no part of her real legs. Every few seconds she reached down to scratch some spot on her thigh where the old, too-tight prosthetics kept rubbing.

"Are you coming?" she asked.

"I'll be right there."

"I'm almost done, anyway," she said. She went back into the kitchen.

I shook my head, trying to clear away my grogginess, and then absent-mindedly felt my back pocket to make sure the acceptance letter was still there. I half expected it to be just another dream, but the paper crinkled through my jeans. Real.

Willa's phone buzzed on the coffee table. I picked it up and read the caller ID. *Benson.*

"Why is Benson calling you?" I asked her.

She stuck her head in the doorway. "What?"

"Benson from the diner is calling you." I walked into the kitchen and started drying the sizable pile of dishes next to the sink.

Willa looked at me sideways. She finished washing the last pan and handed it over. "We only know one Benson, so you don't always have to say *Benson from the diner.*"

"But he *is* from the diner."

"But he's also from, you know, school. Life. Our AP algebra class."

"Well, Benson from our AP algebra class is calling your phone."

She dried off her hands and made a face that was almost impossible to read. It could mean a lot of things. Like:

I should have put my phone on silent, or

I know you were counting in your sleep, or

I'm glad you still have bad dreams, Louis, because I blame you for everything. This is all your fault.

Except what they told me over and over—what they insisted—was that my sister's accident was nobody's fault. And sometimes that made it better and sometimes it made it worse. It made it worse because there was no one to blame and I ended up blaming myself a lot of the time. It made it better because it was just as much her fault as it was my fault. Maybe even more her fault because I think she said it first, I think it was technically her idea (although I've never confirmed this with her for obvious reasons), I think the words left her mouth first—*Let's hang out the window, Louis; let's go out on the fire escape.*

It was really hot. We were eight. I was playing with a toy helicopter, and Willa was fanning herself with a magazine. My mother was cooking dinner in the kitchen, and we didn't have air conditioning so the hot air from outside mixed with the hot air from the stove and we baked alive in the living room for as long as we could stand it and then Willa had the idea to go out on the fire escape and so we did.

We were never explicitly told not to go out there. My mother had neglected to specifically forbid us and that is the loophole we found when Willa came up with the idea and I agreed to it and we opened the living room window and pulled our small bodies onto the ledge and sat with our legs dangling off the side over traffic. I had my helicopter in my hand and I kept buzzing Willa's head with it, and it was cooler and there was a breeze and we were happy, happy, happy. . . .

Until we weren't.

Until Willa twisted wrong and lost her balance and

went over the side and landed on the ground below with a sound I often hear in my nightmares, a sound that wakes me up at night and follows me into the shower and whispers me awake in the mornings and breathes into my ear during breakfast, lunch, and dinner. Every waking moment I hear the heavy, deep crunch of Willa hitting the ground, landing half on the street and half on the sidewalk. And then that sound is followed by the sound of the skidding tires, the squealing brakes, the aggressive pops from Willa's bones as the small navy-blue Honda Civic rolled over her legs in quick succession. One after the other. But that part didn't hurt her, she later told me, because she was already gone. She was floating up above her body. She was next to me on the fire escape. She was watching me watch her die.

My sister, Willa, was born three minutes and eleven seconds before me.

She did not die when she hit the pavement.

She did not die when the car crunched over her legs and hips, crunch, crunch.

She died *a little* in the ambulance, rushing to the nearest hospital where they would try and fail to save her legs, eventually cutting them off with a bone saw I was not allowed to see but imagined to be enormous, cartoonish, taking two doctors to work, one on either side of her pulling and pushing back and forth.

She died for three minutes and eleven seconds, and that has always been the strangest coincidence I can think of. Like somehow she timed it on purpose. Like somehow she was fucking with me.

Willa woke up three days after the accident. She had no more legs. They'd been sawed away.

It was only me in the room at the time.

My mother kept leaving to call my father, who was trying to make it back to Los Angeles from a buying trip in India. My father is Indian, and he and my mother (who is not Indian) own one of the biggest fabric stores in the garment district downtown.

Willa woke out of an induced coma. They stopped giving her the drugs to keep her under, and they told us she'd be along shortly. I thought that was a truly strange way to put it: *she'd be along shortly.*

When she woke up, she looked at me and then she looked down at her body and then she said, "Something's missing."

"Willa, it wasn't my fault," I said.

We were eight, and that seemed like an important point to establish.

"Arms," she said, raising her arms an inch off the bed.

"You had an accident," I told her, which is what the doctors had told me to say.

"Legs," she said. I could see her concentrating on something. Her brain was telling her legs to move but her legs were gone and nothing was happening. She raised her head a little, and I knew she saw where her body ended now, where the sheets dropped dramatically after her thighs.

"It was a really bad accident, but you're okay now."

"I know what's missing," she said. Like she had figured it out.

She fell back asleep for a few more hours.

The doctors told my mother the fall wouldn't even have hurt Willa that badly, but the Honda Civic fractured her femur, which severed a major artery, which required the placement of tourniquets, which required her legs to be cut off, one after the other.

The next time Willa woke up we were all there, my mother and my father, who had finally made it back to Los Angeles and smelled like an airplane when he hugged me. I wanted to say, *I'm fine, Dad. It's her you need to worry about.* But I didn't. Because then Willa woke up and we were all hovering around her bed and the first thing she asked was what had happened to the lower half of her body, thanks very much.

"They saved your life," Mom said.

"They took my legs," Willa said.

"My poor little baby. I'm so happy you're okay."

"I'm not OKAY," Willa said. "I DON'T HAVE ANY MORE LEGS."

The nurse came in and gave her medicine through a tube in her arm.

She fell asleep again.

"It's for the best," the nurse said.

"You can't make her sleep forever," I said.

Or at least that's what I think I would have said, if I could have caught my breath.

My sister had to learn how to walk again. Her first pair of prosthetic legs was small and looked fake—like a child's drawing of what prosthetic legs might look like. The doctor taught her how to put them on and take them off and then gave her a pair of crutches with half circles that went around her arms to help her manage them.

"I don't like these at all," she told me later, kicking the legs off. They landed with a thud on her bedroom floor.

"Why not?" I asked her.

"They're not fooling anybody," she said. And then she lay back on her bed and fell asleep. I picked up her legs and felt their weight and smelled them and they smelled like a new car, or like plastic, or some combination. I stood them up but didn't like how they looked and so then laid them down carefully next to the bed.

I left her alone and had my first panic attack on the floor of our guest bathroom. Of course I didn't know it was a panic attack at the time. It felt like I was dying. It felt like my lungs were burning up inside my chest. Every breath was sharp and impossible.

It felt like something I deserved.

Years later, when Willa had fully adapted to life without legs and mostly got around with prostheses and sometimes, if she was tired, a wheelchair, we were sitting on her bed.

It was hot. Summer.

She showed me a picture in a magazine.

A girl surfing.

"That looks fun," she said. "I wonder if I could do that."

And I said, "I wish it was me. I wish it was me instead of you."

The first time I ever said that.

And she said, "No you don't. Because I've never been relieved it was me instead of you."

She bumped me with her shoulder.

I thought how maybe it wasn't good, how honest we were.

I thought maybe it was sometimes better to lie.

I remember the day my sister lost her legs in almost perfect clarity. The sounds and the smells and the spinning lights of the ambulance and my mother crying and calling my father's phone over and over, even though he was on a plane to India and couldn't answer.

But what I remember most is the toy helicopter I brought

onto the fire escape. I remember that it was there and then it wasn't there. In an instant. My sister lost her legs, and I lost a plastic toy.

I wasn't that concerned at the time, but as the years went by I realized that was only the first of many things I would lose.

After that . . . sometimes it felt like everything I touched was bound to disappear eventually.

THREE
Frances

After I found the bill for the coffin, I went inside and handed it to my grandfather, who was watching TV. Then I went into the kitchen and poured myself a glass of juice. Then I texted my cousin, Arrow (who lived next door), and told her I didn't really feel like coming over to eat the artisanal popcorn her mom bought while watching the *Buffy* marathon on FX. I waited for her response until I felt eyes on the back of my head.

They were both there, my grandparents, watching me, nervous, their hands darting around and touching various parts of their bodies because they didn't know what to do with them. Their hands looked like birds. I wanted to punch each of them in their faces, and this shocked me, because I generally considered myself to be nonviolent.

"Frances," Grandpa Dick said. He held the bill from Easton Valley Rest and Recuperation Center for the Permanently Unwell in his hands. He also held a stack of letters. They were bound together with twine.

"You better have a real fucking good explanation for this," I answered.

Grandma burst into tears. She left the room. She came back into the room. She left again and came back again and then did it so many times in a row that I just forgot about her and turned my attention to Grandpa Dick.

"Listen, Frances," he said. "It's not what you think."

My grandmother came back and sat down at the table next to me. She put her hand on my hand and smiled weakly.

"We are so sorry that you had to find out this way," she said.

"You told me my mother moved to Florida," I said. "You told me she bought a condo in an over-fifty-five gated community."

"We were trying to protect you. We thought it was the best thing," Grandma said. "We did everything wrong. We did everything backward. I can see that now."

I saw the stack of letters in Grandpa Dick's hands. "What are those?" I asked, pointing.

"These belong to you," Grandpa said. He pushed

the letters across the table. I untied the twine and sifted through them.

"Read them in order," Grandma said.

"These are from my mother," I said.

"Yes," Grandpa Dick said.

"My mother wrote me letters?" I said.

"Yes," he said.

"My mother wrote me letters, and you didn't let me read them?" I noticed they were already open. "But you did?"

"For your own good," he said.

I looked at the stack of letters. I turned one over. I turned another over.

They were all addressed to me. They all had the same return address.

"My mother wrote me letters from an insane asylum," I said. It felt a little bit like my brain was processing things too slowly.

"They don't call them that anymore, Frannie," Grandpa said, proud, like he knew something PC that I didn't.

"Rest and recuperation center," Grandma whispered.

"And then she died," I said.

They looked at each other.

"When did she die?" I asked.

"Two days ago," Grandma Doris said. "We were waiting for the right time to tell you."

"You never get the mail," Grandpa said. "How come you got the mail?"

"How did she die?" I asked.

"Frannie, I hardly think that's—"

"How did she die?"

"She hanged herself," Grandpa said.

"Oh, Frannie," Grandma said.

I tried to say something, but my voice caught in my throat. Not a sob really, but something harder. "I could have gone to see her," I whispered.

"It was complicated," Grandpa said.

"It doesn't seem complicated," I said.

I stood up. I stacked the letters on the kitchen table. In the correct order. I didn't think I wanted to read them yet.

But I took the bill with me. It felt like I had earned it.

Later, Grandma Doris came into my room and sat on the edge of my bed. Grandpa Dick stood in the doorway. He had the letters in his hand, but he held them away from his body. Like he didn't want them close.

"I should have known," I said.

"You couldn't have known, Frannie."

"My mother hated Florida," I said. "She refused to take me to Disney World. All my life I just wanted to go to Disney World and she wouldn't take me."

"We'll take you to Disney," Grandma offered. "We'll take you and Arrow. I never knew you wanted to go."

"What about the spider?" I asked. "There wasn't a spider, right?"

"We didn't want you to get her letters, Frannie," Grandpa answered. "Your mother was a very sick woman. We thought you'd had enough crazy parents for a lifetime."

"I'm really, really mad at you," I said.

"We just love you. And we were only trying to do the best thing for you," Grandma said, patting me on the knee.

"Did you ever read the letters?" I asked.

"Oh, they all say the same thing," Grandma said. "We used to read them, Frannie, but there's only so much we can take."

"And now she's dead. My mother is dead," I said.

"My daughter is dead," Grandma said.

"My daughter-in-law and my stepdaughter is dead," Grandpa Dick said.

The weird thing about my grandparents is that they are both my paternal *and* maternal grandparents. In a non-incestuous way. Grandma Doris is my mother's mother and Grandpa Dick is my father's father and when each of their respective spouses died twenty years ago, they cut their losses and married each other. Which is weird, sort of, and maybe not weird, sort of.

"What was wrong with her?" I asked. "I mean what did she . . ."

"Schizophrenia," Grandma said. "Late onset. She had a psychotic break. She never recovered."

I couldn't help picturing my mom in a straitjacket, in a hospital bed with straps holding down her arms and ankles.

A small mound of pills placed into a tiny white paper cup.

"Can I have some time alone now?" I asked.

"Of course you can, sweetheart," Grandma said.

"Take all the time you need," Grandpa said. Then he paused and looked a little sheepish and said, "Did you take the bill? I'll trade you."

He held the letters out to me and I reached for the bill, which I had put on the nightstand, but it wasn't there.

This didn't surprise me.

It was just another thing that disappeared into the void. It was there and then it was gone. It had melted away or else poofed into smoke—I don't know. I had never actually seen something vanish.

"I don't think I have it," I said.

Grandpa put the letters on my nightstand and then they shuffled out of the room, one after the other.

I leaned back on my bed.

I took the first letter out of its envelope.

Dear Heph. Ugh, what a drag. They search EVERY-WHERE when you get here. Not sure it's even legal, I'm looking into it. I have a very good lawyer, and he is telepathic like me! Maybe love?

I put the letter down and considered my options.

I could throw the whole stack away. I could pretend my mother was still living in Florida. I could pretend today was a day like any other day. A normal, whatever day.

But of course I couldn't do that.

My mother was dead and she had written me all these letters, and now I had to read them.

Oh! By the way! I never told you this, but your father isn't really your father. Your father is Wallace Green, the movie star. They don't have any of his movies here, which is a downright shame. I think Nightingale at Midnight is my favorite, but then again, Charming Town is also very good.

You're probably wondering why I never told you this and of course the answer is: I didn't want you to think less of me. I cheated on your father with Wallace Green, one blur of a weekend spent living like somebody I wasn't.

Of course I entertained the idea of not going back to your father. At that point I knew he couldn't have kids (he didn't know; I tore up the test results) and I really, really wanted one. I wanted you, you know, although I didn't know what you would look like or how you'd come out or what you'd be like or who you'd love or how you'd like to wear your hair. I didn't know anything about you, but I felt you even then, this little ball of potential inside of me that I couldn't give up.

That's why I cheated on your father, I think, or

at least a part of it, because back then I still did love him and I really hoped with all my heart that they were wrong and he could give me a baby and we could figure out a way to live the "happily ever after" dream that I so wanted for myself.

In the end I think I went back to him because I was scared. I didn't know how to leave him. I didn't know how to start over. And of course, Wallace Green wasn't offering me a new life either. He was just offering me a weekend, and I took that weekend with everything I had and made it last so I could replay it in my head whenever I was feeling blue.

But then just about two months after those two days together I figured it all out. . . . The sleepiness, the missed periods, the bloating, the cramps . . . And then YOU, seven months after that. And you were everything I wanted, Frannie, really. More important than the Hollywood dreamboat or the piles of money, more important than how I was beginning to discover, even then, Frances Senior's nasty temper. Oh, Frannie. It was all about you, from the very beginning. I hope I made that clear enough before I had to go away.

Anyway, I love you very much and hope you're being good. I'll write soon! —Mom

Oh. Okay. No big deal. It was only a posthumous letter from my mother telling me my father was actually a famous movie star. If anything, her letters would probably shine some light as to why exactly she had been committed to the center. I could deal with that.

I carefully set the first letter down on the bed and picked up the second.

Heph—I have to apologize for my last letter. The doctors here are very nice but a little tricky. And I told them I didn't want medication and they told me I should probably have medication but instead of swallowing it I only hid it under my tongue. Like Wallace Green did in the movie <u>Patient Thirteen</u>. Remember we watched that together so long ago? I probably shouldn't have let you see it because it's a little scary. But you were always hard to rattle.

But it turns out I SHOULD have taken the pills the doctor gave me because I was, as they have explained to me, in a "manic state," which makes it hard to tell if the decisions I'm making are the right decisions or the wrong decisions. I'm referring of course to telling you that Wallace Green was your father. I mean, I think you have the right to know, but maybe I should have eased you into it.

At any rate, I'm sorry, but it is true. Wallace Green is your father. He is a very nice man, or at least he was when I knew him.

I guess sometimes I wish I hadn't married Frances at all. I wish I had married Wallace, and I wish we had raised you together on a ranch somewhere in the middle of nowhere. I wish we had given you a brother or a sister, and I wish we could spoil you into the ground, pour money over you until you were buried in it.

I don't think Frances ever knew about my weekend with Wallace Green. I was always very careful to keep it a secret from everybody because I've known from a very early age that you can't trust anyone.

Oh, Frannie. I don't know. Maybe I should have stayed with Wallace. Maybe I should have buried you in money. You know they say that money changes things. But it wouldn't change how much I love you because I love you an unchangeable amount. —Mom

They went on like that for pages and pages.
I kept reading till dawn.

FOUR
Louis

I woke up early the next day and checked my nightstand drawer immediately. The acceptance letter was still there, but I wouldn't have been surprised if it wasn't. Like the helicopter, the things in my life had a tendency to be there one minute, gone the next.

But there it was, right where I had left it. I unfolded it and read it over again, making sure I hadn't made up the part where they'd accepted me on a full scholarship.

Included in the envelope was a letter from the head tennis instructor. She had invited me to come down to take a tour. *Anytime,* she'd written. *You are welcome anytime.*

I put the letter back in the drawer and closed it. I leaned

back in my bed, struggling to keep my breathing under control. Just reading the letter, just considering the possibility that I might actually get to play tennis for a Division I school . . . it was enough to make me feel anxious and like I was running out of air.

I hung over the side of my bed and rescued my laptop from the floor, where my cat, Bucker, was currently sleeping on it. I checked my email first, scanned Facebook, and then headed over to TILTgroup.org, a site that hosted online support groups for people who'd experienced tragedy.

In the years after Willa's accident, we were both sent to therapists.

We had back-to-back appointments with an older woman, graying hair twisted into a thick, neat bun. My sister went first. I read outdated issues of *Highlights* while my mother knitted erratically. My mother knitted so much in the year following the accident that she had to have surgery on her wrist. One of her tendons swelled up so big it was like an enormous fat worm underneath her skin. Afterward, even though the doctor said it was okay, she wasn't so interested in knitting.

"It was nobody's fault," the therapist often said to me.

But because she said it so often, I had to assume the opposite.

We saw Dr. Williams for a few years, but when we got a little older, she suggested we sign up for accounts at TILTgroup. It was a way to wean ourselves off therapy without quitting cold turkey, she said, and plus it was sometimes easier to open up from behind the safety of a computer screen.

"This is progress!" she exclaimed to the both of us in our separate sessions. "I am so happy with all the work you've put into therapy!" (She often said the exact same things to each of us. We compared notes after our appointments.)

Except apparently Willa was making more progress than I was, because a few months after we started TILTgroup, Willa was released from face-to-face therapy. Dr. Williams recommended that my parents keep me in both, at least for the time being.

Dr. Williams told my parents she was concerned about my insomnia.

She told my parents she was concerned about my panic attacks.

She told my parents a lot of things that I wish she hadn't told my parents, because they started looking at me like they were worried I was going to lose it, snap in half, or explode in the living room.

Post-traumatic stress disorder. A propensity for self-harm.

Willa and I heard her because we stood on the opposite side of the door, eavesdropping.

"What's *propensity*?" Willa asked.

"I don't know," I said.

"What's *self-harm*?"

"I don't know; shut up."

I was irritated because Willa didn't have PTSD. I was irritated because Willa was the one who had lost her legs but I was the one stuck in therapy.

"Your daughter is a surprisingly well-adjusted young lady," Dr. Williams told my parents.

"I'm well-adjusted," Willa whispered.

"She just feels bad for you because you don't have any legs," I told her.

"Well *you* have to keep seeing her and *I* don't."

"CB," I told her.

That was what we called all the special treatment Willa received for being a young kid with a handicap. CB stood for chair benefit. Like when we went to Disneyland and we didn't have to wait in any of the lines, or how we always got to park closest to the mall, or how any type of concert or show sat us directly in front of the stage. I got to benefit from all of Willa's CB, of course, because when she got free ice cream in Universal Studios, they couldn't just not give free ice cream to her twin brother.

So it worked out for both of us.

It didn't make up for the accident. Obviously.

But sometimes it felt like Willa had lost her legs, and I was losing everything else.

• • •

TILT stood for *Tragedy Inspires Love and Togetherness*.

You were supposed to call yourself a tragedy overcomer.

Years later and it still didn't feel like I'd really overcome anything. I also hadn't actually attended a group session in a while, but I still logged on to TILT daily. I mostly just used the messaging feature, because the one good thing to come out of TILT was my best friend.

Whose real name I didn't know. She went by the screen name TheMissingNib.

It was kind of weird but I don't know—it also kind of worked.

Besides not knowing her name, I also didn't know exactly where she lived (East Coast somewhere. Maryland maybe? Rhode Island?) or what she looked like (it was against TILT policy to exchange photos). So for all I knew she could be an old, weird serial killer and not the teenager she claimed to be.

But I liked talking to her, so to be honest, I didn't worry that much about anything else.

I was planning on telling her about my acceptance to the University of Texas, but my password kept failing. I was terrible with passwords. I tried a variety, one after another:

Bucker

Buckerisacat

Buckermcbuckerson

Nothing worked.

I had them email me a reset code.

When asked to pick a new password, I typed in *Buckerisnowmypassword*.

The site labeled my password *weak* but accepted it, so I was feeling fairly triumphant as the home screen popped up.

I had one unread message from TheMissingNib.

It's six in the morning over here. I've just spent the past five hours reading every letter my mother's written me over the past five years. You know, my mother who moved to Florida? Except—and here's a fun new fact I recently learned—SHE NEVER MOVED TO FLORIDA. She's been living in my town the whole time, IN A MENTAL INSTITUTION. WTF. Except now she's dead. Are you awake? Message me when you're awake.

I checked the clock. It was about seven in the morning. Nib had sent the message four hours ago. I hit Reply and typed back:

I'm awake now. Are you?

I hit Send.

Her response popped up a minute later.

I'm awake. Instamess?

TILT didn't have instant messaging. I opened up the Instamess application on my computer. I was still signed in from last night, so I closed my away message and opened a chat box with TheMissingNib.

BuckerMcBuckerson // Hi.

TheMissingNib // Hi.

Bucker // Hi. I'm so sorry about your mother.

Nib // I thought she was in Florida. This whole time.

Bucker // I can't believe your grandparents lied to you for so long.

Nib // You and me both. I thought they were benevolent, but it turns out they are evil old people and must be destroyed.

Bucker // She wrote you letters?

Nib // Like a ton of letters. At least once a month for five years.

Bucker // What do they all say?

Nib // They're mostly crazy. Unintelligible. I mean, she was in the nuthouse. She didn't really have all her faculties.

Bucker // Do you mind if I ask you something . . .

Nib // She hanged herself.

Bucker // That's terrible.

Nib // Hanged is the correct verb, btw.

Bucker // I know.

Nib // You live in LA, right?

Bucker // Yup.

Nib // Guess who my mom says my real dad is?

Bucker // Who?

Nib // Wallace Green.

Bucker // The actor? For real?

Nib // I mean, we must take that with a grain of salt. She spent the last five years getting lobotomies, probably.

Bucker // Well he doesn't even live in LA. He lives in Texas. I think I read that in a magazine.

Nib // All the movie stars are moving to Texas.

Bucker // Yeah. Isn't it 4 AM where you are?

Nib // We're three hours forward, not backward. You're not very good at clocks.

Bucker // Oh, yeah. I knew that. Have you slept yet? Maybe you should get some sleep.

Nib // Trying to get rid of me?

Bucker // I have to drive my sister to the doc.

Nib // Everything OK?

Bucker // She's getting fitted for some new legs. She wants to be taller.

Nib // Really?

Bucker // Ha. No. She doesn't really fit the old ones anymore. These will probably be the last pair, though.

Nib // Forever legs.

Bucker // That's a snappy name. I might call her that.

Nib // Don't tell her it was from me. Talk later.

Bucker // Bye, Nib.

TheMissingNib has disconnected.

I threw up an away message. *Life is beautiful. For some more than others. (Fishing with John.)*

I closed my computer and got dressed. I usually only showered at night because I couldn't get into bed unless I felt clean.

I left Bucker sleeping on the bed on my laptop (I don't know what it was, he just really liked sleeping on my laptop) and walked down the hall to Willa's room. Her door was still closed, and I didn't bother knocking before I pushed it open.

She was sleeping on her back, one arm draped across her eyes, her mouth opened and turned toward the wall. The covers were pooled down at the bottom of the bed. She couldn't kick them away, so she would sit up and throw them off her. She was always hot. She had two fans blasting on her. It made me uncomfortable. I didn't like the noise or the blades. My mother used to say we'd chop our fingers off. Then she stopped saying that.

"Wake up. We're going to be late," I said. I started pulling clothes out of Willa's bureaus. It was easier if I picked her clothes out for her. Not because she couldn't do it, but because she didn't like to.

It might be weird to say this, but my sister is fairly beautiful. I'm not saying it in a creepy way, I've just heard it repeated so many times that I finally had to acknowledge its truth. She has thick, shoulder-length brown hair, light eyes, and clear skin. Everybody talked about how beautiful Willa was but nobody said it to her face because she didn't like to hear it. She didn't care.

And we're twins, sure, but we don't look anything alike. The male equivalent of Willa would be a movie star or, like, a famous model or something. I am neither.

"Skirt or shorts?" I asked her.

She never wore pants. She couldn't walk as well in them, and she didn't like covering up her prosthetics.

"Let them fucking stare, who cares," she always said. And she wasn't just saying it to say it. She really didn't care. She was the least self-conscious person I'd ever met. Losing her legs hadn't changed that.

"How hot is it?" she mumbled. "It feels hot."

"I think it's hot."

"Skirt. And bring me my legs."

"Get your own legs," I said. I threw her a skirt and a gray T-shirt and she pulled herself to a sitting position. She swung her thighs over the edge of the bed. She was wearing an oversized Mickey Mouse T-shirt and bright-pink sleep shorts. Her hair was sticking up on one side.

"It's hot," she said.

"You don't have time to shower."

"Where are we going?"

"Dr. Brightman."

"New legs," she said. She reached for her old ones and started pulling them on. "These are starting to pinch."

"Good timing, then."

"I thought Mom was taking me?"

"She's at the store. Big client or something."

"Is Dad back yet?"

"Flew in last night. You were already asleep."

"I'm still tired," she said.

"Well, you can take a nap later. Right now we have to see about some new appendages."

"I hope they match all my shoes," Willa said.

She had one pair of shoes. Gray Converse. I threw them at her and left her to get dressed.

Even though I had just talked to Nib, I wrote her a short message while I waited for Willa to finish getting ready.

Just wanted to say sorry again, about your mom. I can't really imagine what it feels like and I guess I just wish I could do more for you. Sometimes it sucks, being internet friends—like I wish I knew your address so I could send you a card or something. Or flowers. I think flowers are a nice gesture. Please imagine I have just sent you a very large bouquet of flowers. You can pick what kind. The card attached should say something sweet but not overly sappy. Something appropriate but heartfelt.
Like—I'm thinking of you. (Not in a weird way.)
—Your strictly internet friend, Bucker

Given the circumstances, I decided to wait on telling her about the University of Texas. I put my phone in my pocket and thought maybe I would tell Willa instead. But then she came out of her bedroom with her eyes still closed and ran directly into a wall, so I thought maybe it could wait.

Besides, I wasn't sure I was ready to tell anybody yet.

For some reason it felt like it had to be a secret, like maybe if I said it out loud it would become real. And so many real things disappeared.

FIVE
Frances

I slept from ten in the morning until eleven in the morning and then I rolled over and grabbed my phone off the nightstand.

I read a message from Bucker. I closed my eyes and imagined a bouquet of flowers sitting in a vase on my bureau. I wrote him back:

> Something appropriate but heartfelt. I like that. I think it
> speaks for itself. And thank you for the flowers; I think I
> might be allergic, but it was a nice gesture.

I pressed the button on my phone and said, "Call Arrow."

"Who would you like me to call?"

"Arrow."

"Okay. What would you like me to do?"

"Call Arrow."

"Okay. Would you like to send Arrow a message?"

"Go fuck yourself."

"That is not a valid—"

I turned off my useless robot and dialed my cousin's number myself. She answered after the fourth ring. Clearly asleep.

"Why did I watch six hours of *Buffy* by myself last night?" she said.

"I have a very good explanation for that."

"And I would love to hear it in, I don't know, three hours? Call me later?"

"Can I come over? I'm gonna come over."

"I don't think so. I mean later, sure. Come over later. Right now is not a great—"

"I'll see you in few."

I hung up on her and got dressed quickly, running a brush through my hair without looking in the mirror.

Arrow lived just next door. I let myself in the back. My aunt Florence was chopping veggies in the kitchen. I felt like my aunt Florence was always chopping veggies in the kitchen.

"Hi, Frances! What a nice surprise."

I came over every day, multiple times a day, and Aunt Florence was always nicely surprised to see me.

"Hi, Aunt Florence."

"Did you have breakfast? I have oatmeal made! And all manner of accoutrements."

Aunt Florence generally used words like *accoutrements,* but she didn't generally cry while chopping veggies, so that's how I knew she knew. She was my mom's sister, after all.

"You know about my mother, huh?" I said.

Aunt Florence put her veggie-chopping knife on the cutting board and wiped her hands on her apron. She always wore aprons, and I had never seen her wear the same one twice, which led me to believe she owned too many aprons.

"Oh, honey. I'm so sorry," she said.

"I'm sorry too. And I'm sorry everybody lied to me," I said. Then I shrugged and got a bowl of oatmeal and went upstairs.

Arrow was sitting cross-legged on her bed, her eyes closed and her breathing deep. Morning meditations. I didn't know where she'd picked it up from, but she meditated every morning and night. She said she wasn't herself if she skipped a day. I sat at her desk until she was done. I ate my oatmeal.

Arrow was adopted from Vietnam when she was three

years old. She had short straight hair and yellow-rimmed glasses she used for reading. She was wearing bright-pink shorts and a bright-yellow top. It didn't strictly match.

When she opened her eyes, I said, "You don't strictly match."

"Well, you're in a fun mood," she said.

"I am not in a fun mood," I said. I took the last bite of oatmeal and placed the bowl on the desk.

"Did my mom make oatmeal?" Arrow asked.

"Yeah. Oh, my mother is dead," I said.

"What?"

"My mother died. She killed herself in an insane asylum. Here. In Easton."

"I'm not following," Arrow said.

"My mother never moved to Florida. She was here the whole time. She was committed."

Arrow thought for a moment. Then she said, "Easton Valley Rest and Recuperation Center for the Permanently Unwell?"

"How did you know that?"

"I wanted to volunteer there, but my parents wouldn't let me. It would have looked amazing on my college application. I couldn't understand why they were so against it."

"They didn't want you to see her," I said.

"That is a new level of shadiness." She slid off the bed and crossed the room and hugged me tightly. I rested my head on her shoulder. Her skin smelled like lotion and soap and for some reason it made me want to cry. I hadn't cried yet. My chest was knotting up. "I'm so sorry, Frannie," she said, pulling away. She sat down on the edge of the bed.

"It's okay. I'm okay."

"I can't believe they lied to us."

"This whole time, I could have just gone and seen her," I said.

"I don't get it," Arrow said. "I just don't get it. I can't believe she's dead."

"You know, she wrote me all these letters. I always wondered why she didn't write to me, and she had. I just never got the mail."

Arrow's eyes widened. "The black widow spider."

"There aren't even black widow spiders in Maryland."

"You know, I could never picture your mother living in an over-fifty-five gated community in Florida," Arrow said thoughtfully. "Everybody told me she had some kind of midlife crisis, but my mom has had plenty of those and she's never moved south."

"I thought she just didn't want me," I said. My voice broke awkwardly. Arrow looked at me and waited.

"I guess this is better, right? This is better?" she asked.

"She's dead, Arrow. What's better about being dead?"

"Oh, Frannie. Please don't cry," Arrow whispered. She scooted closer to me and grabbed my hands. She leaned so far over the side of the bed I thought she'd fall off. "I can't remember the last time I saw you cry."

"I'll cry if I want to," I said.

"Let's get some more oatmeal. Let's watch a movie. Let me paint your nails."

"I don't want you to paint my nails. I want to cry."

"Frannie, please, please, please don't cry. I love you so very much and we can do anything you want to do other than crying, okay? Anything you want to do. Do you want to go to the beach? Do you want to go paddleboarding? You keep saying you want to try paddleboarding!"

Arrow was starting to tear up. I knew she didn't want me to cry because she cried all the time, because even the word *cry* made her want to cry, because she had no control over her tear ducts and considered them traitors to her otherwise stoic demeanor.

I tried to pull myself together. I closed my eyes and took a few deep breaths. When I opened my eyes again, Arrow was staring at me. Her own eyes were wide and nervous.

"They all said the same thing. Her letters. I spent all night reading them," I said.

"What did they say?"

"I mean, my mother is crazy. Was crazy. So, you know. How much can I really believe?"

"What do you mean? Believe what?"

"She kept talking about Wallace Green," I said.

"The movie star?"

"She said he's my real father."

"The movie star?" she repeated.

"Yes, the movie star."

"Do you believe that?"

"Of course I don't believe that."

"She really said that?" Arrow asked. She moved an inch away from me and squinted, studying my face. "You don't look like Wallace Green."

"I don't look like my father either," I said. In truth, I was the spitting image of my mother. If it was possible for a person to have sex with themselves, to get pregnant by themselves, to have an immaculately conceived baby, then that was me. There was nobody else in my face. Just my mother.

"I brought this," I said, pulling my mother's last letter out of my pocket. It was dated just last week.

"Is that . . ."

"Yeah."

I handed it to Arrow and then read it over her shoulder, even though I had already read it a dozen times. I'd read all of them a dozen times.

> Heph—Some days are easier than others, some days are almost inbearable. Unbearable? I miss you a lot, but it's okay that you haven't written because you shouldn't have to carry this burden around with you. The burden of words. It wouldn't be fair.
>
> The man in the top hat came back to see me and told me a very important secret about the bedsheets

here. Oh, Heph, I wish I could see you one last time, but I could never get the hang of astral projection. It's unfortunate because it would have been so useful, all those nights I missed you so much I couldn't sleep.

All I wish for you is that you find Wallace Green because I never had the guts to. I was comfortable with Frances the First and thought that following my dreams might only ruin them or worse, I'd come to realize that our dreams are never what we think they are.

You are the stuff of stars and you deserve to have a real father, not a coward who tried to kill you.

All my love. Mom

"Jesus," Arrow said when she had finished.

"I know."

Arrow got off the bed. She turned a few tight circles in the carpet and then looked at me, worried.

"Are you going to?"

"Going to?"

"Find him? Wallace Green?"

"Of course not." I paused, thinking back to my conversation with Bucker. Bucker wasn't his real name. I didn't know his real name because I'd never asked because it didn't matter. He was just a screen name. He could have been a fifty-year-old convicted felon. He could be instamessing me from a jail cell. I think he said once that Bucker was his cat, but Bucker could just as easily have been his cellmate. "He lives in Texas, I guess."

"Texas is far from here."

"Well, yeah. It's halfway across the country."

"How do you know he lives in Texas?"

"TILTgroup."

"Someone on TILT knows Wallace Green?"

"Well, he knows where he lives, I guess."

Arrow was still standing. She was playing with the ends of her hair, making miniature braids and unbraiding them. I'd always been jealous of Arrow's hair. It was stick straight and thick. Even when they'd brought her home (an event I only vaguely remembered, and probably only because it was on videotape somewhere), she'd already had that hair. It grew at an alarming rate. She got a trim every other week.

"I'm really sorry, Frannie," she said after a minute. "I loved your mom so much. She always had those little butterscotch candies in her purse. I almost choked to death on one because she let me eat them in the car. And she was funny, you know? She was really funny."

"And she was really crazy," I added.

"Sure," Arrow said. "But look around you. Everyone is."

"You're not crazy."

"My mom is probably crazy. I mean, they're cut from the same cloth and everything. And you've seen how many veggie platters my mom makes. Like, who are all these veggie platters even for? What does she do with them? They're there and then they're gone. I certainly don't eat them."

"She takes them to her book club," I offered.

"Sometimes I think there's no book club," Arrow said.

"So where does she go all the time?" I asked.

"Oh."

"What?"

"Maybe she takes them to your mom," Arrow said softly.

"Oh."

For some reason, picturing my mom eating veggie plates in a mental hospital was the last straw.

We cried together for hours, and when we were done crying we went and ate the veggie plate Aunt Florence had left on the kitchen counter, not even because we particularly wanted it but because it felt, in a weird way, like a tribute.

When we were finished, Arrow went to take a shower and I snuck into my aunt and uncle's room. I took the photo album from Aunt Florence's vanity. Arrow and I used to look through this album when we were kids. It was pictures of the two of them, Florence and my mom, when they were younger.

I didn't have any photographs of my mother. She had burned them all one afternoon right before I went to live with my grandparents. We sat in the backyard and she put a match to every single one. Burning pictures smell terrible. Like something poisonous and wrong.

I removed a photo from the album—a picture of my mother by herself, her hand held in someone else's hand, a man's hand, his arm cut off by the edge of the photo so it was just my mom being led somewhere by someone without a body. He wore a thick silver bracelet with a chunk of turquoise in it. My mom looked up at the camera and laughed, laughed, laughed more than I had ever seen her laugh in real life.

I took the photo and put it into my pocket.

But when I looked for it later, it was gone.

SIX
Louis

It was hot, even for Los Angeles. We were in the middle of a heat wave, one hundred and five degrees in June.

"You need a shot of Freon," Willa informed me, leaning close to the air ducts in my car. "This is like bathwater. This is like someone blowing on my face. It isn't cold at all."

"It just needs a second."

"We've been driving for ten minutes. How much longer does it need? A shot of Freon is three dollars. Go to Jiffy Lube. I'll treat."

I didn't know what Freon was or whether I wanted it in my car, but I didn't say anything to Willa. She was one of those people who seemed to know everything about everything, but I never saw her online or reading books or the newspaper so I wasn't sure where she got her information. It was like it appeared, magically, in her brain, and that was annoying, because everything I read or studied or learned, I forgot. She had a better grade point average than I did, and I don't think I'd ever even seen her crack a textbook.

"You don't know what Freon is, do you?" she asked.

"Of course I know what Freon is," I said.

"What is Freon?"

"I don't have to tell you what Freon is."

"Because you don't know. I mean, that's fine. Some people don't know what Freon is."

Freon is a word that sounds less like a word the more you say it.

Freon.

Freon.

"Are you hungry?" I asked. "We have time to stop, if you want."

"I thought you said we were going to be late. Isn't the appointment at eight? It's five of eight."

"It's at eight thirty."

"You lied to me?"

"For your own good. Sally's?"

"Fine, but I'm not going in, because that was deceitful. I want an egg sandwich with avocado. And tater tots."

I pulled into the diner's parking lot a few minutes later.

We went there a lot. They were fast and clean and close to our apartment.

Willa reclined her seat and closed her eyes. I left the car on for her and stepped out into the blazing sunlight. The air conditioning was definitely working; it was easily twenty degrees hotter outside the car. I started sweating instantly. You would think spending my entire life in Los Angeles would mean I was a little more accustomed to the heat. Nope. I dreamed of snow. I'd never even seen it. I think I would like to ski.

I opened the door to the diner. Benson, the owner's son, was at the host's stand. He was short and stocky; he played football on the school's team. I didn't know anything about football, but I think he was good? People said he was good. He was pretty popular, but one of those popular kids who was also nice. A rare combination.

"Hey, Louis," he said when I opened the door. He looked behind me and asked, "No Willa today?"

"She's in the car," I answered.

"Oh," he said. And maybe his face fell a fraction of an inch, or maybe I imagined it. I thought he probably had a crush on her, but I knew lots of guys who'd liked my sister only to have their hopes dashed when they found out she only had crushes on sleeping and tater tots. And plus—if she liked Benson, I was pretty sure she would have told me.

"Can I put in a takeout order?"

"Sure thing. Usual?"

"Usual would be great."

"I'll throw in some extra tater tots. I know she likes them."

Benson scribbled our order on his pad and went to give it to the kitchen.

I pulled out my phone and read a message from Nib. It made me smile—she had received my fake flowers. I typed her back while I waited for Benson. We usually wrote back and forth a few times a day, just checking in, small stuff. But because of what had happened to her mother, I felt even more of a need to make sure she was okay.

It's hot in Los Angeles today. I think this guy in my school might have a crush on Willa, which is very OK with me. He gives us free tater tots! Not just like randomly—he works in a diner. Anyway, hi. Is it hot there? Are you OK? Take an allergy pill for the flowers.

I put my phone back in my pocket as Benson returned with two coffees to go.

"Thanks," I said, taking them.

"No problem. So where are you headed? The store?"

Willa and I worked part time at my parents' fabric store. It was about as thrilling as it sounded. Willa cut fabric all day, and I was on restock. It was miserable, but our parents were entrepreneurs and had this great need to instill the same drive in Willa and me. We would inherit the shop one day, and my mother had already made it clear she would come back as a ghost and haunt us until the day we died if we ever sold it. I've heard the "we started that store from the ground up" speech too many times to count.

"We'll be there later on. Willa's got a doctor's appointment."

"Everything okay?"

"New legs," I said.

Maybe it was weird how nonchalantly everyone talked about Willa's accident, but despite it being downtown Los Angeles, there was actually a small-town, community feel in our neighborhood. Everyone knew us, everyone knew Willa, and everyone knew my mother was passionate about two things: tulle and normalizing her daughter's lack of legs. Willa was never bullied or treated differently. It maybe helped she had the attitude of a long-haul trucker. Nobody wanted to fuck with her.

"That's great! I know her current ones were getting a little old."

"Sure. I don't know. I guess these will be the last ones for a while. The doctor said she's done growing."

Willa would have been tall, had it not been for the accident and subsequent transfemoral amputation. Her torso was long and narrow, and you could just tell by looking at her that she was supposed to be a giant. I was tall, anyway, and we were twins.

"There have been huge strides in prostheses over the last few years," Benson said thoughtfully.

"I guess. I don't really pay attention."

"It's fascinating. You should do some research."

I couldn't think of anything less interesting than researching the kind of fake legs my sister had to wear, but I nodded and tried to look engaged. I mean, clearly Benson was into it.

The order-up bell dinged and Benson went to get our food. "Tell Willa I said hi," he said, handing me a paper bag. I struggled to carry it with the two coffees.

"Sure, will do. See you soon, Benson."

I shouldered open the door and was hit with a wave of heat so powerful I was surprised it didn't light the bag on fire. Willa was currently leaning against the window with her eyes closed. I tapped on the glass and she jolted, instantly irritated. She rolled down the window, and I handed her the bag and her coffee.

"Benson has a crush on you," I said.

She rolled her eyes but not before I thought I saw a flicker of something else. Embarrassment? Disbelief? "Benson does not have a crush on me. Oh, why—did he give us extra tater tots?"

"Exactly."

I walked around the side of the car and put my coffee on the roof while I pulled the door open.

"Well, that was nice of him," Willa said slowly, staring into the bag.

"Is everything there?" I asked, sliding into the car and shutting the door behind me.

"Everything's here."

"Then why are you being weird?"

"I'm not being weird."

"Why are you staring into the bag like that?"

"I'm not staring into the bag like anything, shut up."

I put my seat belt on and shifted the car into reverse, maneuvering out of the parking space slowly.

"Maybe I'm being weird because I'm going to get new legs," Willa said finally. "I've had these ones for years."

"Well, you said they pinch you."

"A lot of things hurt, but that doesn't mean you won't miss them when they're gone."

"How philosophical."

"I'm just saying. Getting new legs kind of sucks. You have to learn how to walk all over again."

I shifted into drive and merged into traffic. Willa popped a tater tot into her mouth and then handed one to me. It was really the perfect tater tot. They'd perfected the art of totting taters.

"Did you not get a coffee?" she asked, taking a sip of hers.

"Oh, fuck," I said.

"The roof?"

"The roof."

I looked in the rearview window. I was expecting to see my coffee, laying broken and spilled in the middle of the road, but it wasn't there. So I pulled over and looked on the roof, but it wasn't there either. I got back in the car.

"Here. We can share." Willa handed me her cup.

"Thanks." I took a sip and burned my tongue.

It was too hot for coffee anyway.

"You have something on your mind," Willa said after a minute.

"Me?"

"No, the other person in the car I might possibly be talking to."

"I don't have anything on my mind."

"You've been acting weird since yesterday. You know, after you fell asleep instead of doing dishes and then looked at my phone like a creep."

"I didn't look at your phone like a creep," I said.

"You were counting in your sleep, and I know you only count when . . ." She trailed off. It wasn't easy for either of us to talk about. She had told me once that sometimes when I did it, she could feel something scratching at her skin. Sometimes when I had panic attacks, she could feel herself not breathing.

"I wasn't counting."

"Your lips move," she said, and demonstrated. I watched her out of the corner of my eye. "It's okay. You can talk to me about it. You can tell me if it's happening again."

"Nothing's happening. There's nothing to talk about."

"Okay, Louis. Just know that I'm here. Or whatever. If you want to talk. Or whatever. I don't even care."

She ate another tater tot.

I found myself thinking about what Austin might look like. The University of Texas had a campus there and that's where I would go. If I decided to go. I mean, I hadn't decided yet. I had never even been to Texas.

I wondered if it could possibly be hotter than Los Angeles in the summer.

I wondered if I could possibly move so far away from home when even normal things like sleeping and washing dishes were sometimes hard for me.

I didn't know.

But I did know that no, Texas couldn't possibly be hotter than Los Angeles. Any hotter than this and we'd be burned alive.

SEVEN
Frances

After I took the photograph of my mother from Aunt Florence's photo album, I went home to take a shower. I always took really hot showers and I always forgot to turn the fan on beforehand, so the bathroom filled up with steam and my grandpa yelled at me because the wallpaper was peeling off and I was going to cause a mold outbreak. My skin turned bright red and my fingers wrinkled and Grandma Doris complained about the hot water bill.

"It doesn't pay itself, you know," she always said.

But Grandpa Dick had been a colonel in the army, so I know they're fine with money. His pension is absurd. My grandmother carried Chanel handbags and wore Prada sunglasses. But all her clothes came from T.J. Maxx, so I guess it evened out.

I took an extra-long shower and toweled off in a bathroom cloudy and wet. I made a circle in the mirror, wiping away the condensation with the palm of my hand. I looked tired and red. I wrapped the towel around me and opened the door. Steam poured into the hallway.

"Frances, really," my grandmother said. She was standing at the top of the stairs, clucking her tongue.

"You told me my mother lived in Florida," I said.

"That's hardly related to our water bill," she replied. But she left me alone.

I went into my room and that's when I noticed the picture of my mother was gone. I had put it on my pillow and now it wasn't there.

I touched the spot where it had been and it felt warm but that was probably because the sunlight streamed in through the window and fell across the bed like an invading army of light.

I got dressed quickly. It was June and hot but the muggy, thick air couldn't make it into our house. Grandma Doris apparently didn't care as much about the electricity bill; we had central air and it was always blasting.

I sat on my bed and opened my laptop. I checked TILTgroup first. After the pen-stabbing incident I had been sent to therapy, where my therapist told my mother I should also be utilizing support groups. Since my mother was generally insistent we do everything we could possibly do in the name of my mental health (which seems ironic now), she signed me up for my very own TILT account. At first I used TILTgroup for weekly guided-support groups, but now it was more like a habit. I never attended group sessions anymore. I only had a few people I private messaged, and I only really liked Bucker. We had clicked from the beginning, from one of my very first sessions. Most of the other kids there just wanted to talk about their tragedy. They were less like overcomers, Bucker had said once, and more like dwellers. When Bucker talked about his tragedy, he was really talking about his sister, and he was never weird about it. I liked that. He didn't give up his whole life because something shitty happened to him. He didn't surrender his identity to TILT just because some therapist had asked him to. I hoped I was like that too.

TILT.

Tragedy Inspires Love and Togetherness

We found other possibilities for the acronym:

Totally Ignorant Losers Talking

Translucent Illusions Leaving Town

I signed in and went to my messages.

Just one from Bucker about how hot it was in LA.

I wrote him back quickly:

It's hot and muggy here. Is it muggy in LA? It's not, right? You guys are lucky. Mugginess is the worst. I'm trying to figure out if I should do something really stupid. Like, drive-across-the-country-to-meet-a-movie-star stupid. I keep going back and forth.

I closed my laptop and lay back on my bed. I was glib with Bucker, but the truth was that my stomach had tied itself up in a knot that felt irreversible. The truth, Arrow and I had cried for a long, long time, but I didn't feel like I was done.

I loved my mother. I missed her. Admittedly, I missed her more five years ago, when it was fresh, when one day I had spent all my time with her and the next day she had vanished, poof, never to be heard from again. I had learned to live without her, but that didn't make the pain any less real.

But I knew even then. I knew after my father went to jail and it was just my mother and me, spending money on stupid things and getting our hair done twice a day at different salons. I knew it couldn't last forever. I was only a kid, but I could see my mother unraveling. I could see the knots in her brain unknotting. She was falling apart. She was coming unhinged.

She burned our pictures and smashed in our TV set to make an aquarium.

"I don't want a TV anymore," she'd said. "I want a fish tank. Put these safety goggles on, Heph."

I put the safety goggles on. I stepped back until my butt

hit the far wall and then I watched my mother take a bat to our television. It wasn't a flat-screen; it was one of the old ones.

My mother bashed the shit out of that poor TV and then she stepped back and looked at me like—e*h? Pretty cool, huh?*

"I've never seen the inside of a TV before," she said, bending down and inspecting it. "Come here and look. It's like a science experiment. Don't worry, I unplugged it."

I went and looked at the inside of the TV. To be honest, it was a little boring.

"What kind of fish do you want?" she asked me.

"Goldfish?"

"How many?"

"Three?"

"Names?"

"I dunno."

"Heph! They gotta have names."

"Goldy?"

"Inspired. And the others?"

"Sunshine. Lava."

"I love those names *so much*," she said, putting her arm around me. "All we have to do now is saw the top off and get a sheet of glass. We'll go to the hardware store later, how about it? We need a saw and we need some glass and we'll probably need some netting for the top. Like a screen. So they don't jump out."

We never made it to the hardware store.

I missed my mother now. Her letters were manic and nonsensical and long-winded, but they made me miss her in a way I hadn't missed her in five years. They made her feel so close. I was happy she had thought about me in the mental institution. I was happy she wrote me letters even when the letters were filled with made-up words.

Tole barken! she wrote in one of them. *Howba goesy!*

I wanted to read them again even though I was so tired my eyes burned with the effort of staying open. I'd left them on the nightstand this morning when I'd finally fallen asleep. I reached over to get them, but they weren't there. They had gone wherever the photo of her had gone. They had gone wherever everything went.

I knew I wouldn't find them, but I got up anyway and went downstairs to the living room. Grandma was knitting something on the couch. She wasn't supposed to knit anymore, because of her arthritis, but she didn't listen to the doctors.

"Did you take my mother's letters?" I asked.

"No, dear. Did you misplace them?"

"I know where I left them. Maybe Grandpa?"

"Grandpa's been gone all day."

"How come you lied to me? I mean, really," I said.

"Oh, Frances." Grandma Doris put her knitting down. She took a deep breath and rubbed at her temples. "Do you really want to know?"

"Yeah, I really want to know."

"I didn't want you to grow up worried."

"Worried?"

"Your father was a nutball," she said. "Don't tell your grandfather I said that, but he was a certifiable nutball. After he got out of jail, he tried to get custody—"

"I know all that."

"And he was laughed at. The judge laughed. *You don't get to stab your daughter with a fountain pen and then file for custody*, the judge said. Your mother got a restraining order, and we never heard from him again. And good riddance."

"I don't know what that has to do with anything," I said.

"I didn't want you to grow up thinking you'd go crazy too. With your father being who he is, and your mother in a special hospital . . ."

"Oh," I said. "You know, it hadn't occurred to me until just now."

"Well, good. That was the whole point."

"I read all her letters."

Grandma rubbed her right hand with her left. "And what did you think?" she asked.

"She says my father isn't my father."

She nodded slowly, like she knew already, and I realized she had read them all even though she said she had given up after a while. I wondered if my mother had written letters to her too, or if that was reserved for me. "Wallace Green,"

Grandma said after a minute. "I always liked him."

"But you don't think . . ."

"That he's your real father? Oh, honey. I don't think so."

I sat down on the armchair. "You're probably right."

"I'm sorry we lied to you, Frannie. And I'm sorry we kept those letters from you. I hope you know we did it because we love you more than anything."

"I don't forgive you."

"Well, I guess I can live with that for a little while."

"You know she told me she wanted me to find him, right?"

"I know," she said sadly.

"And you don't think I should?"

"I don't think it would help anything."

I went back upstairs.

I felt divided. Half of me wanted to believe my mother, to prove her right, because it would show that she wasn't completely gone. It would prove that there was a part of her that was still sane, still able to reach me.

But the other half of me wanted to forget everything she'd told me about Wallace Green. No good could come of it. There was no way he was my father, and that road could only lead to more pain. My mother was dead, and she believed something that wasn't real.

I sat down on my bed.

The letters had not reappeared.
I was always losing things.
But no, it wasn't me.
Things kept leaving.
Things disappeared.

EIGHT
Louis

Willa ate the tater tots in the parking lot of the doctor's office. It was time to go inside, but she was stalling. I didn't think I'd ever seen my sister nervous before and so I couldn't be sure that was what this was. But she ate each tater tot so slowly and she looked at each one so deeply, like it might contain the answers to all the questions of the universe, including the most pressing one of how to stall for time before going into a doctor's appointment.

"Willa?" I said finally.

She looked at me like she'd forgotten I was there. "What?"

"Are you nervous?"

"What would I be nervous about?" she said quickly. She looked into the bag, but I guess she'd finished the tater tots because she crumpled it up and threw it on the floor of my car.

"Uh, your legs?" I said.

"I don't have any legs," she said, flashing me a wry smile and opening the door.

It was hard for her to get out of cars. She had to use her hands to lift her feet over the door. Then she gripped each side of the doorframe and pulled herself out.

I didn't help her unless she was really tired. It only made her angry.

I turned off the engine and grabbed Willa's coffee cup. It was still half-full. I met her around the back of the car.

"I meant your new legs," I said.

"I know what you meant."

"So, are you?"

"Nervous?"

"Nervous, yeah."

"No, Louis, I'm not nervous about my new legs."

"So you're nervous about something else?"

Willa stopped walking. She turned her face up to the sky and closed her eyes behind her sunglasses.

"Why are you being so nosy?" she asked.

"I'm just trying to help."

"I don't know. I guess I'm tired. I don't think I got enough sleep."

In the waiting room, the receptionist asked her to fill out a new emergency contact form.

"I do one of these every time I'm here," Willa argued. "Literally nothing has changed. It's still my brother. Somehow, in eighteen years, I've managed to not make any better friends."

"It's policy, love," the receptionist said. She knew Willa. She winked at me. "Six months between visits, you gotta fill out a new form."

"How come you don't have iPads yet? I could do all this on an iPad. It's greener," Willa complained.

"Okay, love, I'll be sure to give the doctors your feedback: *Willa Johar is tired of paper forms.* I've made a note of it here on my space pad."

"It's not a space pad," Willa mumbled, taking the clipboard the receptionist was wagging at her. "It's an iPad." She grabbed a pen from a black plastic holder and sat down next to me.

"Hey, cranky," I said.

"This is asinine," she retorted. "Your phone number hasn't changed. Our address hasn't changed. This is a waste of paper."

Definitely nervous. I watched Willa fill out the form, noting her severely shaking hands and shitty penmanship. At the bottom of the paper, she wrote, *Go green.* Then a nurse came and called her name and she dumped the clipboard on my lap. I set it on the chair next to me.

I watched her disappear behind the waiting room doors, and I wondered what they'd do with her old legs. I couldn't remember what had happened to the ones before these. Maybe they donated them to people who couldn't afford their own?

I pulled out my phone and opened up the TILTgroup app, which was terribly designed and had zero functionality besides checking times for different support groups and reading your messages (if you were lucky, and it didn't make your phone crash).

I had a message from Nib, a quick one about taking a road trip to find Wallace Green.

I pressed Reply.

Willa had asked me once why I liked talking to someone I'd never met. At first I hadn't known what to say, but it felt like I knew enough about Nib. She told me about her family. I told her all my secrets.

And it was safe too. I couldn't find her. She couldn't find me. She was just a screen name.

Nib—I'm sitting in the waiting room of the doctor's office, waiting for my sister to get her new legs. She got fitted a few months ago, but they take a long time to make. They're state of the art, supposedly, and they're setting us back an absurd amount of money. But my parents' store is doing really well, I guess. They were featured on that reality show about making clothes? I don't know. I wasn't allowed to be in the episode because I "didn't promote the brand." That's what my mom said. That's kind of harsh, but I also didn't really want to be on TV anyway. I left my coffee on the roof of my car and then drove away. That is my tragedy for the day. Do you ever feel like everything disappears? I am trying to find a way for my coffee's disappearance to inspire love and togetherness, but really I just feel irritated. Hope you're doing well. Your tragedy of the day is worse than mine, admittedly.

–Bucker

I finished the message and pressed Send, then locked my phone and slid it into my pocket. My sister's appointment wouldn't take long. They'd show her how to put the legs on and they'd make sure she could do it by herself a few times, and then we'd be on our way. My mom was supposed to take her, but then one of our biggest clients had some sort of Egyptian cotton emergency. Willa and I had been back and forth to the doctor's so many times over the years (leg fittings, leg adjustments, general leg health) that we were fine on our own.

I was tired. Willa's coffee was lukewarm, and she took it without sugar. I liked one packet, the brown kind. I had a sip of hers, but it was too bitter. I sat back and closed my eyes.

I didn't fall asleep but I drifted in and out of a weird place until my sister leaned over me and tapped me on the shoulder. She didn't look happy.

"Behold," she said. "My new transfemoral prostheses."

I looked at her legs. She lifted her skirt a little to oblige me.

"They look the same, really," I said.

"They feel weird," she said thoughtfully. She lifted one leg, then the other, testing them. She swayed a little. I grabbed her arm. "I'm supposed to use a walker for the first couple weeks."

"Do you want me to get it? Is it still in my trunk?"

"LOL if you think I'm actually using a walker," she said, rolling her eyes. "I'll be fine. Plus, so what if I fall? It's not like they can re-amputate my legs."

"Well, I think they look nice."

"You said they looked the same."

"They look the same. I mean, they look newer."

"They are that."

I stood up. I put my hands on her shoulders. "Wait. Are you taller?"

She smiled and shrugged. "I don't know. Am I?"

"You are! They're taller!"

"Well, if I still had my real legs, they would grow too," she said. She tried to turn around gracefully and almost fell sideways. I put my hand on her arm. "Did you give that form to the nurse and decide you liked the clipboard too much to part with it?"

"What?"

Willa picked the clipboard up off the chair. It was

empty. Its little clip was only clipping air. She showed it to me, shaking it to demonstrate its lack of paper.

"I didn't . . ." I hadn't touched it. I looked underneath the chair and behind the chair and then I said, "I have no idea. I didn't touch it."

"Great. Now I have to fill out another fucking form or else face the wrath of the receptionist," Willa said, rolling her eyes. "We might as well just find a forest somewhere and burn it or something. All this paper. It's depressing." She took the clipboard to the front desk and filled out another form. She was a little shaky. I helped her out to the parking lot.

She'd described it once as walking on stilts. But they were stilts that were suction-cupped to your body. It was basically impossible to slip out of them, so if you fell, they fell with you. When she'd been fitted for her first pair, she used to worry about becoming detached. But the weight of her body, as she later explained it to me, kept them in place.

It just took a lot of work. You had to lift up one leg at a time. I could see her concentrating. And I knew when she got too tired to do it. She couldn't stand up all day. At school, she took wheelchair breaks. At home, she sat down a lot.

I think that was part of the reason she slept so much. She was almost always concentrating on not falling over. It must have been exhausting.

"I have to get used to you, like, three inches taller," I told her. We were about the same height now.

"Two inches," she said. I opened the passenger door for her, and she sat down heavily. She looked exhausted. I moved to lift her legs into the car, but she batted me away.

"I have a portable in the trunk," I told her. "I'll get it out when we get to the store." Portable wheelchairs weren't comfortable, though. There might be a better one at the store.

"Only our parents would make me work on brand-new legs," she mumbled.

I shut her door and walked around to the driver's side. I watched her put her seat back. I knew she wished she could drive, but it was either new legs or hand controls for my Corolla. We couldn't afford both.

We'd tried it once, in the lot of an abandoned warehouse building (there was no shortage of abandoned buildings downtown). She'd only been at it for thirty seconds before she ran my car straight into a telephone pole. Luckily, we'd been going about five miles an hour and she'd happened to hit the exact spot my car had been backed into just a week before (by our probably legally blind neighbor who was ninety and definitely shouldn't have been parallel parking anymore).

My parents would flip if they knew I'd let Willa behind the wheel. But she kept asking and asking and finally I let her.

"Hey, Willa?" I said, ducking into the car.

"Yeah?"

"You know Wallace Green?"

Willa snorted. "Do I know Wallace Green? Do I live in the world? There are posters for that new robot movie fucking everywhere."

The Day They Came, starring Wallace Green and Saige Firth. Opening date: July 8. Robots gain sentience. Take over the world. Etc. Something about aliens.

"Yeah. You know that girl I talk to on TILT?"

"Yeah," she said. "The pen girl."

"Yeah."

"What about Wallace Green?"

"Her mother died. The girl on TILT. And I guess she wrote her all these letters insisting that Wallace Green is her real father."

Willa snorted again. "Okay. I mean, that's hysterical. Wallace Green, long-lost father. I mean, it's obviously not true. Her mother sounds crazy."

"I don't know. I think he lives in Austin?"

"Again—why do I care?"

"I was just having a conversation with you. This is how conversations work. Each person takes turns saying things."

Willa looked over at me, but I kept my eyes on the road. Willa was always difficult, but it seemed like there was something else going on now.

"I'm sorry," she said.

"Whatever."

The truth was—I wanted to talk about Austin because

that was where the University of Texas was, and that was where I was possibly going to school in one year and two months, give or take, on a full scholarship.

The thing is, I'm really, really good at tennis.

My dad took me on the courts for the first time when I was just three years old. I beat him at singles. He thought it was funny, so he invited a couple friends. I beat them at doubles. And then I kept playing, and I kept beating people. And when I got older, since our high school didn't have a tennis program, they shipped me to the Pacific Palisades, a much wealthier school district (more money = more tennis). I beat everyone in the Pacific Palisades, and then I worked my way up and down the coastline until I had beat everyone in Southern California. And then the University of Texas sent people to watch me play, and those people offered me a very early, very generous, very prestigious scholarship to come and play for their NCAA Division I tennis team.

And the campus was in Austin.

And Wallace Green was in Austin.

And that couldn't help but feel like some sort of divine gift. Or, at least, a pretty cool coincidence.

I had no idea what to do.

Aside from not even knowing whether I'd be able to handle the pressures of going away for school, I was also worried about my parents.

On the one hand, they'd be thrilled.

We weren't poor by any means, but we weren't exactly swimming in money. It was expensive to raise a daughter with no legs, and it was expensive to live in downtown LA, and it was expensive to fly all the way around the world looking for new fabric. And the store was doing well (*Project Runway*? Is that a thing? It had been on TV, I don't know), but sending two kids to college in the same year was really stressing my parents out. I'd heard them talking about it.

So a full scholarship—they'd be overjoyed.

But a full scholarship in Texas—I wasn't so sure.

My mother didn't even like it when I went to the Pacific Palisades by myself, and that was thirty minutes away (or, like, twelve hours, depending on traffic). I couldn't imagine what she'd say if I told her I wanted to go to school in Texas.

And then there was Willa.

I'd never been away from her before.

People talked about twins being spiritually connected or whatever, and sometimes it was bullshit but other times it was true.

Like when Willa fell off the fire escape and lost her legs, I could feel it.

I could feel a tickle in my thighs as the bone saw cut her legs away. My knees got numb and my toes cramped up and I couldn't walk. For one full hour, I sat in the waiting room and couldn't stand. I lost the feeling in my feet. I could tell the exact moment they brought bone saw to bone. I knew when it was over. I could feel them stitching her up. It might as well have been me.

We had never been apart. We had never talked about what we were doing after graduation. We'd be starting senior year soon, and I had no idea what Willa wanted to do after that.

For eighteen years it had been her and me.

I didn't know how to tell her it might not be that way forever.

And just thinking about the possibility was making it hard to catch my breath.

I pulled into the parking lot behind our parents' store, into one of three parking spots marked Private, No Parking. I turned the engine off and reread the message from Nib as Willa let herself out of the car.

Was it the stupidest idea in the world, to travel across the country to meet a girl I hadn't even seen a picture of? Was it the second-stupidest idea? If it was the second-stupidest idea, what was the first stupidest? Thinking I could move across the country to play Division I tennis at one of the best schools in the country?

I kept going back and forth. They seemed equally stupid, I thought. And maybe not stupid at all. If I was honest, they seemed maybe a little perfect.

But were they *too* perfect?

Ugh. I couldn't trust my brain to be positive for more than a few seconds at a time. I got out of the car and took

Willa's portable wheelchair from the trunk. I wheeled it around to the passenger side; she grumbled when I woke her up, but then let me help her into it.

"You're counting again," she said as I pushed her toward the back entrance of the store.

She was right.

Lately I was counting a lot.

Lately I couldn't seem to catch my breath.

NINE
Frances

I had not yet decided whether I would go to my mother's wake.

I knew I should, but it was hard to talk myself into it. It would be small, just me and Grandpa Dick and Grandma Doris and Arrow and Aunt Florence and Uncle Irvine and my mother's coffin being lowered into a plot in a local cemetery that apparently she had purchased twenty years ago, because that is a thing people do that I didn't realize people did. But it made sense. I mean, you can't buy a burial plot when you actually need it.

Two days had passed since I'd found the bill for the coffin (the bill had never turned up, but I had no doubt they were already printing another one), which meant my mother had been dead for four days and the local funeral parlor was putting pressure on us to make a decision. I knew this because they called at least once a day, feigning sympathy for our deceased loved one and saying things like "Sometimes the best way to begin the healing process is to go through with the burial rites."

I was still angry with my grandparents, but I was beginning to understand their reasoning.

Bucker and I had been talking a lot, exchanging multiple messages a day and debating the pros and cons of driving halfway across the country to meet each other while attending to our own complicated quests.

Just a few minutes ago I'd gotten this:

Maybe we can actually call it a quest, though? I think that would help. I think that would make it cooler.

I'd responded:

I think that would make it nerdier.

I felt my phone buzz now and took it out to find a picture he'd sent me: Gandalf in full wizarding gear. I wondered if Bucker was maybe a forty-year-old man with a sizable collection of Games Workshop armies. (I mean, not that I was complaining. I kind of liked that idea.)

I wrote him a message:

Are you more down with regular Warhammer or Warhammer 30,000?

He wrote back immediately:

It is Warhammer 40,000, and none of the above. I obviously like the Tolkien series the best.

I was drafting him a reply when the doorbell rang. I found Arrow on my doorstep in running clothes. It was seven o'clock in the evening and getting dark. She had a nylon backpack with running clothes for me, spandex shorts and a sports bra and a thin tank top. She pulled my hair into a ponytail and handed me a terrycloth headband.

"I don't particularly feel like running," I said. I sat on my front steps and laced up my sneakers. "I feel like we've had this conversation before."

"I usually run with Addison, you know. But she's away for the summer. I don't like to run by myself. Safety in numbers."

Arrow had always been very concerned with safety. She watched a lot of crime shows on basic cable.

We ran.

I hated to run, and after only thirty seconds it was a struggle to convince my legs to keep moving. Arrow might as well have been in the bathtub for how relaxed she looked.

"You're doing great," she coached. "Just focus on the next step. You can always, always run just one more step. Don't think about anything except for that next step."

But what was the next step? Did I agree to have a wake for my mother? Did I want my last visual memory of my mother to be her lying in a casket? Or did we have a closed casket?

My knees protested the exercise, and my lungs started to burn. I was out of breath and we hadn't even been at it for two minutes.

"Decrease your speed, but *don't stop*," Arrow instructed.

I decreased my speed.

I missed Addison.

"The goal is to keep your heart rate up while finding a maintainable pace," Arrow continued.

"I think my maintainable pace might be *stopped*," I said. I decreased my speed again. I'd developed a sharp kink in my left side. I held my ribs while I ran.

"It takes practice," Arrow said. She was running backward now, facing me.

"I'm sorry," I gasped. "It must be really annoying to have to go so slow."

"I don't mind," she said. She turned sideways and started doing weird skip-steps.

"Are you not even breaking a sweat?"

"I don't sweat that much," Arrow said, shrugging. "But

you know, Frannie, we all have our things. I'd love to be able to draw."

"I'm not even that good at drawing," I said. "I hardly do it anymore."

"You're not doing anyone any favors by selling yourself short. You're an amazing artist."

"Maybe," I said. I was panting.

Arrow smiled and said, "Come on. Let's go back. We'll do some cardio in the front yard. Do you have a jump rope? I can get one from my place."

We ran by the light of the streetlights. We were maybe ten minutes out and I forced myself to speed up again, to match Arrow's pace. Arrow turned backward, sideways, skipped and sprinted ahead, circling back. She could be reading a book. She could be cooking dinner. She looked utterly unchallenged.

We fell silent. I thought about my mother, about my father(s), about Bucker and his sister. I thought about tragedy, I guess, how unfair it was that we weren't doled out the same amount. How some people get so much and some people get none at all.

That's what I was thinking when I saw the figure dart up behind Arrow and grab her around the waist.

Arrow screamed—I screamed—but then Arrow laughed and I stopped so suddenly I tripped and fell down, hard, on my knees and wrists.

"Ow," I mumbled into the sidewalk.

"Oh my gosh—*Frannie*!" Arrow shrieked, doubling back and dropping to the ground beside me.

I was panting but Arrow looked practically serene. The shadowy figure skipped over to us.

"Use the four steps," I whispered. My hands were warm and wet; I was bleeding.

"The what?" Arrow asked.

"The four steps to disarm your opponent. Like we learned in gym class."

Arrow laughed. "It's just Hank."

"Hank?" I said.

"Hank Whitney," Hank Whitney said.

"Oh. Hi, Hank Whitney." I vaguely remembered Hank Whitney from Arrow's track team but didn't think we had ever actually spoken before. He always seemed to be running; I would have had to yell.

"Hi, Frances Jameson," Hank said, grabbing me around the wrist and heaving me up before I could protest. "You're bleeding."

"Yeah. I guess I am." I put my hands on my knees and bent over. "I am also out of breath. I am possibly suffocating."

Hank was wearing running shorts and sneakers and a white T-shirt. My heart, beating a hundred miles an hour with exertion and the sudden positive fear I was about to be murdered, struggled inside my chest. I breathed in through my nose and then tried to breathe out through my mouth but only ended up coughing.

"Here," Hank said. He reached into his pocket and pulled out a perfectly clean, perfectly white handkerchief. He used it to staunch the blood on my palms, which was sort of substantial.

"You run with a handkerchief?" I asked.

"For sweat," he said, shrugging.

"Ah. Arrow doesn't sweat."

"Well, we're not all biologically perfect creatures like Arrow," Hank said. "She's basically like a cheetah."

"I'm like a tortoise," I offered. "A slow, bleeding tortoise."

"Do you think you need stitches?" Arrow asked, taking the handkerchief from one of my wrists and moving my arm around until it caught a beam from a streetlight.

"I think she's fine. Just some soap and Band-Aids," Hank said. "Keep the handkerchief. Sorry I scared you, Frannie. Can you make it home okay?"

"Sure, Hank," Arrow said.

"Thanks, Hank," I said.

He saluted us goofily and turned on the spot, running away with the sudden speed and grace of a cat.

"He's kind of creepy, right?" I asked.

"He's not creepy," Arrow said. She let go of the handkerchief; I pressed my wrists together to keep it secure. "Can you walk?"

"He's sort of—"

"He's just out running. We see each other all the time."

"A handkerchief?"

"That your blood has now undoubtedly ruined. So you sort of owe him one."

We started walking back to my house.

"But I mean—who carries a handkerchief on a run?"

"You're right. Actually—do you have your cell phone on you? We should really alert the proper authorities. Man with a handkerchief and running shoes, undoubtedly up to no good."

"Oh. You're mocking me now."

"Yes," Arrow said. "I am mocking you. You are being easily mockable."

"Great. I get it."

"Hank Whitney is nice," Arrow said, shrugging.

"What?" I said. "Oh my God, do you love him?"

"Yes, I love him. We've been having a secret romance. It's all very clandestine."

"Well, you think he's cute. You're kind of blushing."

"I don't *blush*," Arrow said, like it was something distasteful. "He's a nice guy, I'm just not really interested in anything like that right now."

Arrow had never really been interested in anything like that. I guess I hadn't either. It had never seemed important.

And then when I *did* get the inclination, he ended up living across the country from me.

Which didn't seem all that fair.

Silence. The dusty glow from the streetlights and the buzz of mosquitoes and moths. I was dive-bombed by a small flock of no-see-ums. My hands and knees were burning. I wondered if someday I would wake up just knowing how to be a decent, productive member of society. I wondered if someday all of this would make sense to me. Everything that had happened. Everything my parents did. I wondered why my grandparents lied to me. I wondered if their excuse was good enough. If they deserved my forgiveness. I wondered whether I would have been better off finding an actual black widow spider in my mailbox. One quick bite and then one long paralyzing rush of poison and they'd find me beyond help. Already dead on the driveway.

"Frannie?" Arrow said.

"Yeah?"

"Are you going into shock? From loss of blood?"

"Oh. I don't think so. It's mostly stopped."

"That was super graceful, by the way."

"I was scared. I thought we were about to be murdered."

"Seventy-five percent of murder victims have a relationship with their killer. So I am much more likely to murder you than Hank Whitney. And Hank Whitney is much more likely to murder me than you."

"When you put it that way," I said.

"And of that seventy-five percent, nearly thirty percent are family members," she continued.

"So what you're saying is, I'm actually lucky my mother is dead? Because that lowers my risk of being murdered?"

We had reached my front steps. Arrow sat down heavily, sighing as she did.

"That's terrible, Frannie. That's not what I meant at all."

I sat down beside her. "I'm sorry. I don't know why I said that."

"You're deflecting," Arrow said. "You're using humor to distract yourself from the mourning process."

"Did you hear that on TV?"

Arrow shrugged. "It makes a lot of sense."

The door opened behind us, and Grandma Doris poked her head outside.

"Girls? Is that you? Frannie? Are you bleeding?"

"Jogging accident," I said, showing her my battle wounds.

"Well, you better use some antibiotic ointment. And give them a good wash. Dinner's ready. Arrow, of course you're more than welcome."

Grandma Doris shut the door.

"What do you know about Texas?" I asked her.

"Wallace Green?" she said.

"Wallace Green."

"Do you think . . ." She trailed off, but I knew what she was going to ask. Did I really think there was a chance Wallace Green could be my father?

"I don't know," I said.

"So why do you want to go?"

"Well, I'm not sure if I want to go. But if I *did* want to

go . . . it wouldn't be for him. It would be for her. She asked me to find him, you know. In her last letter."

"I know," Arrow said. "So—what's your plan? If you decided to go, I mean."

I thought for a minute and then said, "'Hi. My mom says you're my father. Will you agree to a paternity test?'"

"Your approach could use a little work. But I'm in if you're in."

Arrow stood up. She reached for my hand and helped me to my feet.

"Thanks," I said.

"It's not like we have anything else to do," Arrow said. She was right. Our plans for the summer included binge-watching old television shows and learning how to sew.

"I'm thinking about it."

"Where'd the handkerchief go?"

I'd been holding it in my hand.

I *just* had it.

But the handkerchief was gone.

Everything I touched was disappearing.

TEN
Louis

I got Nib's next message sitting in Sally's parking lot, working up the courage to leave the air-conditioned car for the hot walk to the entrance.

Bucky, I know I've told you before that I lose things, but I'm worried it's getting worse. I lost the letters my mother wrote to me and a picture of her I took from my aunt's photo album. I lost a handkerchief from a boy named Hank Whitney who runs track with my cousin. And maybe that's part of the reason I want to go to Austin? I mean, I haven't decided. But what if Wallace Green is my father? Then maybe I would have found something pretty big. —Nib

It was getting worse for me too. It had been getting worse since I was eight years old.

It was little things, mostly. Like my parents would ask me to make a delivery, and they would load up the back of my car with swatches of fabric or reams of lace or buckets of buttons. They would count everything and I would count everything because at least two people had to count everything to make sure it was right. That was my mom's policy. And then they would put it in my car and I would drive it to the client's office, and when I got there, inevitably, something was missing.

My mother had accused me once of selling it on the side for drugs. I couldn't even properly defend myself against her allegations because I was laughing too hard imagining me bringing a yard of tulle to the corner and exchanging it for an ounce of weed. Apparently the drug dealers in her imagination moonlighted as seamstresses.

I wasn't selling it, of course. I had no idea what happened to it. It was there and then it wasn't.

It wasn't just fabric. Last school year, I lost my history textbook three times. After that, Mr. Steinbeck would only let me use his spare book in class. I had to borrow Willa's to do any homework (she didn't mind because, like I said, she put her textbooks in a pile in her room at the beginning of the school year and there they stayed, untouched, till June).

Socks. Pens. Tennis balls. T-shirts.

It had been happening since I was a little kid.

Packs of gum. Sunglasses. My wallet. My car keys. Cups of coffee.

Two days after Willa got her new legs, I went to Sally's by myself to pick up grilled cheese sandwiches for lunch. Willa was at the store, my father was in Dubai, and my mother was at a client meeting in Marina del Rey. I wasn't supposed to leave Willa in the store by herself because it was a big store and if we got a rush, she wouldn't be able to help everyone. (This had nothing to do with her legs and everything to do with how needy our customers could be.) But it had been slow all day and we were starving. Mom was supposed to bring back pizza, but her meeting was running hours over because some wedding shop wanted a ridiculous amount of lace, I don't know. She sent me a text full of dollar-sign emojis and then a pizza and then a broken heart and then a little yellow face, crying. My mom was surprisingly well versed in emoji speak. I went to Sally's to get food. Willa had called ahead so it would be ready when I got there.

Benson was manning the host stand as usual. And as usual, he looked behind me when he saw me.

"She's at the store," I said, pulling out my wallet.

"Oh, I wasn't . . ." He stopped, shrugging. "Nothing. Hey, Louis."

"Hey. Just picking up."

"Yeah, I have you." He went over to the counter and grabbed our bag of food, then placed it in front of the register. "Fourteen forty."

I took my wallet out of my front pocket. I don't know if this is interesting to anyone except me, but I kept my wallet in my front pocket instead of my back pocket. I just never liked how it felt in the back pocket, and plus I kept losing it, so I thought I would try something different. And I hadn't lost my wallet for over a year, so things were going pretty well. Until I opened said wallet to remove my twenty-dollar bill from its depths, and there was no twenty-dollar bill.

"Uh," I said.

There was also no debit card, because I'd left that in front of my computer last night (I bought an album, nothing weird). But there should have been a twenty-dollar bill. I had a twenty-dollar bill. I knew I had a twenty-dollar bill because Willa had just given it to me about ten minutes ago. We had transferred it from Willa's purse to my wallet. I could picture it perfectly. It had happened.

"Get me later," Benson offered, handing me the bag.

"This is embarrassing."

"I know where you live," he said, smiling. "Seriously, don't worry about it. Get me later."

"I must have lost, the, um . . ."

"Louis. Chill."

I took the bag from Benson and mumbled thanks.

Willa was going to kill me, not only because I didn't have change for her, but because our fourteen-dollar lunch was now, essentially, thirty-four dollars and forty cents.

From the store to the diner, I had not removed my wallet from my pocket.

Which basically proved my theory that the shit I lost, I didn't actually lose.

The shit I lost disappeared.

On my tenth birthday, just over two years after Willa had fallen off the fire escape, my parents bought me my first nice tennis racket. A Babolat. It was the most beautiful thing I had ever held in my hands.

My father took me to our local courts to play. It was nearing sunset and the city had taken on an otherworldly, mystical quality. I was ten years old and I had the most beautiful tennis racket that any ten-year-old had ever owned. My father cracked open a new, pressurized container of tennis balls, and we listened to the sound it made in the darkness—*whoosh*. We were the only ones on the courts. Three courts lined up next to one another and we were the only ones there, just my father and me. And my new tennis racket, buzzing in my hand. Like an extension of my body. Like a thing alive.

We played for hours. We played until the lights came on and the moths started to gather and the sky darkened to a light gray. There were never stars in Los Angeles. There was never the pitch-blackness of the desert, which I'd seen only once before. The city towered around us, and I beat my father, again and again, and this racket and I became a unit. We became one thing. And I was so grateful that my father was home, because he was such a good father and I admired him so much, but he was just too often not here, he was too often on the opposite side of the world picking through muslin or taffeta or cotton.

And Willa was always getting everything she wanted and now I had gotten what I wanted. This tennis racket.

When we were done, I put my racket into my case and then placed it in the trunk beside my father's racket. My father was holding up the trunk and he watched me put my racket beside his and so he couldn't even yell at me when we got back home and we pulled into the parking garage and he popped the trunk and we walked around to the back of the car and the Babolat was gone. My racket was gone but my father's, of course, was still there, and the balls were still there. Just my racket was gone because everything I touched was disappearing into the void. I knew this at ten, but I was too scared to articulate it.

"What happened to your racket?" my father asked. He held the door to the trunk because it was broken and would crash down on us if he let it go.

"I put it here," I said, and placed my palm on the coarse carpeting. I imagined it, I'm sure, but the place I had put the racket was warm to the touch.

"I saw you put it there," my father confirmed. "And then I closed the trunk. And then we drove home. And then I opened the trunk. And now there's no racket here."

I was already losing things. Matchbox cars. Video games. Shoes.

And I had loved that tennis racket so much already, but I was almost glad it was gone. Because my father was a very level-headed person, and he had seen the racket go into the car and he himself had closed and then opened the trunk, so now he would have to believe me that I wasn't careless with my things. I took good care of my things, but they vanished anyway. Now he would have to believe me.

"The racket is gone," my father said. He moved a few things in the trunk, but the trunk was empty aside from his racket and the container of tennis balls. It was very clear that my racket was gone.

"This is how it happens," I said.

"I saw the racket go into the trunk," he whispered. He wasn't talking to me anymore. I could see the lines on his forehead. I knew he was deciding whether to yell at me or believe me. There were repercussions to both choices.

Finally, I saw his shoulders sag a bit. He ran his hand through his hair.

"That was a really nice racket," he said.

"I know, Dad."

"I guess we left it at the courts? We should probably go back and see, huh?"

"We didn't leave it at the courts, Dad. I put it in the trunk. We both saw."

"Yeah. I guess you're right."

"Now you believe me?"

He looked down at me. He shook his head a little, but then he sighed and nodded. "Of course I believe you, Louis. I saw it myself."

"What are you gonna tell Mom?"

"I don't know."

"But you believe me, right? You have to believe me, because you saw me put it in the trunk. So you have to believe me, right?"

He was freaked out. I knew he was freaked out because of the way his jaw worked. He was grinding his teeth. I was disappointed the racket was gone, but I wasn't surprised. I was used to it.

"I do believe you," he said. "I saw the racket."

"And now it's gone, but I didn't lose it."

"You didn't lose it."

After that, it was my mom who always got mad at me when the things I owned kept vanishing. It was my dad who stuck up for me. He defended me because he'd seen it himself.

I told Willa I'd lost her change. She was irritated, but she didn't say anything.

I don't know if she believed me, about the things I lost,

but she never really questioned me. And that counted for a lot, since my mom assumed I was selling chenille for drugs.

I wrote Nib back:

Maybe we're letting these things leave. Maybe we're complacent. I don't know. I don't know anything.

Willa and I ate the grilled cheese sandwiches at the cash register.

Someone came in and bought two thousand dollars' worth of lampas.

I texted my mom dollar signs and a trophy.

She texted me back fourteen thumbs up.

ELEVEN
Frances

I tried to draw my mother's hands.

I remembered them better than I remembered almost every other part of her: their length and boniness and the skinny fingers paired with cartoonishly large knuckles. I wanted to recreate the photograph I'd lost, my mother's hands wrapped up in someone else's, my mother laughing and throwing her head back, every inch of her body glowing with absolute joy.

But the paper in front of me remained blank.

Arrow was wrong. I couldn't draw.

I used to be able to.

I used to be the high school's star artist; my paintings

and sketches were hung up in the art wing, my signature sticking out in gold. (Why did I sign my name in gold? Was I that materialistic, that full of myself?)

I didn't draw anymore.

One day, toward the end of junior year, I showed up to art class. There was an apple on my teacher's desk. We were between projects, and just about to start our final piece, which would count for 60 percent of our grade. But until then: still life. Our teacher was giving us a break, she explained. A chance to center ourselves. A chance to relax before the piece that would make or break our final grade.

Except I couldn't draw the fucking apple.

I tried.

I mean, at first we all kind of laughed and made fun of the whole apple exercise. We were in advanced art, and we didn't want to draw apples anymore. That was something we had done as freshmen.

So first we laughed and then, after we'd gotten it out of our systems, we started to draw.

We put pen to paper. (Or—everybody else put pen to paper. I put charcoal to paper, because I could never quite get over the twist in my gut every time I held a pen.)

Everyone drew an apple, and everyone's apples were perfect examples of how an apple should be.

Everyone except me.

My charcoal connected to the sheet of clear, clean paper in front of me, and then my hand froze.

Nothing.

I couldn't make myself draw an apple. I couldn't even make myself draw a line. I sat there watching my hand not move and the bit of charcoal not move, and it was like I had forgotten how to tell my brain to make my hand move. It was like I had lost the connection.

Just a couple months before the end of my junior year.

"Draw an apple," our teacher said.

We laughed. We drew.

Except me.

I didn't draw.

I tried to draw, but I couldn't make so much as a single smudge.

"I'll have to give you a zero for the day," my teacher told me when everyone had left. It was just her and me. The paper was still pristine, still white on my desk.

"I understand."

"It was only an apple. Are you feeling all right?"

"Maybe I'm getting sick."

"A zero won't affect your grade at all. It's just for class participation. It will average out. Obviously I expect big things from your final piece."

"I understand."

"You could have drawn something. A circle with a stem on it. Did you see Evan's apple? It's nothing to write home about."

"I tried," I said.

"I'm not looking for Van Gogh here."

"I know."

"Well. We all have our off days."

It was the beginning of many, many off days.

Months of off days.

I couldn't draw anymore. I'd lost that too.

"Do you know Mrs. Tate already has a waiting list? For college recommendations. She's taking names," Arrow said.

Arrow wore a necklace that said *fuck*. But the font was so curvy and elaborate that everyone thought it said *luck*, and she didn't usually correct them. She'd even convinced her mom to buy it for her. She said Aunt Florence had looked at it for a really long time, then looked at Arrow for a really long time.

"Mom," Arrow had told her. "It says *luck*."

"Of course, of course," Aunt Florence had said.

She bought the necklace.

Arrow was playing with it now, pulling the charm back and forth along the silver chain. She was lying on her back on my bed, her feet propped up on my headboard. She had her eyes closed. She was wearing bright-pink eyeliner, expertly applied in a perfect cat eye. It would have looked terrible on me, but Arrow's skin was tan and smooth and she could wear bright colors and they wouldn't wear her, if that made any sense.

"I didn't have Mrs. Tate," I said.

"She's AP American History," Arrow said. "So obviously you didn't have her, because you suck at history. I mean, I'm not even technically American, and I know more about American history than you do."

"You *are* technically American, idiot."

"I wasn't for three years," she argued. "How much do you know about the Vietnamese culture?"

"I know they have a history of making really annoying cousins."

"Rude. Have you asked anyone to write yours?"

"Write my what?"

"Your college recommendations!"

"It's the summer," I said weakly.

"But I said there are already waiting lists! Are you even listening to me?"

I wasn't, to be fair.

I was thinking about my fathers, as I'd taken to calling them.

I hadn't heard from my real father (fake father? Mother's husband?) in years and years and years. When I googled his name, I was really googling my name. So a bunch of websites came back flashing JPEGs of my own artwork.

We were both Frances Jameson, only he was doing a much better job of covering his tracks.

When I googled Wallace Green (real father? Birth father?) I was met with thousands and thousands of websites and fan blogs and image hits and article headers all calling him the "voice of the American people" and "best living American actor" and "super certifiable hunk machine!"

Neither searches were getting me anywhere.

"Frannie. What the hell?" Arrow said, sitting up. She crossed her legs and glared at me.

"What?"

"You aren't listening to me at all. I refuse to be taken for granted. I'm going home. Come over later if you want to watch a movie."

"Arrow, you don't have to go."

"I am removing myself from the situation."

"What's the situation?"

"Being ignored." She hopped off my bed and gave me a quick hug. I was at my desk, my laptop open in front of me.

"I'm sorry," I said.

"Do what you have to do. I'll see you later."

"Arrow," I said. She stopped at the door and turned around. "I'm going to go to my mother's wake. I decided. I mean, you don't have to go if you don't want to, but I think I should. I think I have to."

"I'll need to borrow something black," she said. She smiled and was gone.

I wished I had a better memory. I wished I could remember my mother's letters. But they were long and rambling and incoherent, endless messages scrawled on cheap lined paper.

They detailed the life we could have had, if only she had chosen the movie star over the pen stabber.

I checked the Wikipedia page for Wallace Green. He was famous when my mother claimed to have slept with him, one of those movie stars who are timeless in their reign. His first movie was twenty-five years ago. He was thirty then; he was fifty-five now. He was getting gray hairs. People called him the perpetual bachelor. He was always dating a beautiful woman, but he kept breaking it off just when the marriage buzz kicked in.

My mother was not a beautiful woman, not even when she was younger. She was plain, like me. You don't notice us in crowds. You don't pay particular attention to us. You don't see our bodies or our faces. We don't have pretty eyes or pretty hair. Movie stars don't sleep with us. Not even if they are very drunk. Not even if they are very lonely. It just doesn't happen.

I logged in to TILTgroup.
I had a message from Bucker.
It said:

Nib. Have you decided yet whether you're going to go to your mother's wake? I was thinking about you last night as I was falling asleep. Not in a weird way. I lost a twenty-dollar bill and I remember you saying that your

mother used to think you were hiding things from her but they were really gone, just vanished from this plane of existence. I remember you said that: plane of existence. It made me think of other planes of existence, like maybe there are other versions of ourselves in a parallel universe and these versions are getting the things we lose. I wonder what the other versions of myself look like. I wonder what you look like. Sorry, I know that goes against TILT policy. Totally Ineffective Laboratory Test.
—Bucker

I pressed Reply and started typing.

My grandparents spent five years pretending my mother was someone she wasn't. I don't want to pretend I am anyone other than who I am. You're one of my closest friends, and I don't even know your name. I'm Frances Hephaestus Jameson. You should be able to find me on Facebook. There are pictures and everything. This version of me isn't anything special, but it's better than being called Nib by someone I've known for years. —Frances
P.S. I really hope you are not a forty-year-old internet predator. Or in prison. But if you are either, you have shown truly excellent perseverance in your stalking of me, and I think you deserve this anyway. Take Insane Liberating Trustfalls.

I closed my computer.

I felt weird. But a good weird. Like a releasing sort of weird.

Like I had spent long enough in the dark. Surrounded by lies and dishonesty.

I just wanted to tell the truth.

TWELVE
Louis

Frances Hephaestus Jameson had dark hair and dark eyes and pale skin. She wasn't quick to smile but when she did, it changed her entire face. Not for the better or worse. Just changed. Like a different person.

Her Facebook was bare. Just twenty or so photos of her, most tagged with her cousin, Arrow Pickering. She'd told me about Arrow.

Take Insane Liberating Trustfalls, she had said.

So I sent her a friend request.

And a few minutes later, she accepted.

Then she sent me a private message that said,

Bucker?

I wrote her back:

At your service.

Louis Johar. Louis is a nice name. You look nice. Our
last names both start with J. And you're really eighteen!
Unless you have created a truly elaborate fake profile
with many fake friends and fake photographs. Either way,
I would be impressed!

We can't rule it out.

I'm glad to see your face. Is that weird?

It's not weird. I'm glad to see your face too.

I'm going to my mother's wake tomorrow. And then they're
burying her right after. Closed casket. Just family.

I wish I could be there with you.

I really did; I wasn't just saying it. I didn't have many
friends besides my sister because so much of my after-
school time was spent carting myself to and from the
Pacific Palisades. So much of my middle school and high

school life had been given up for tennis. And for being Willa's private chauffeur.

I wasn't complaining. My schedule just didn't lend itself to making friends. That had never been a priority either. I wasn't secretly bitter about it. I liked being by myself.

But Nib—Frances—was a friend. I told her everything. I remembered the first message she had ever sent me, after one of my very first group sessions on TILT.

Are you really my age or are you lying? Are your parents making you do this too?

I had written back:

Yes and yes.

It had all started from there.
A new message popped up on Facebook.

I wish you could be here too. I don't have many friends.

I don't have many friends either.

You have your sister.

You have your cousin.

I guess only our family members will hang out with us. I think we might be losers, Louis.

Let it be. We don't need 'em.

I have to go. Movie night with Arrow. Text me, if you want to.

And she left her phone number. A 410 area code.

I saved it under *Frances*.

Then I googled the name Hephaestus, and found out he was a Greek god, the son of Zeus and Hera. So I read about Greek mythology for an hour and then I went to see if Willa felt like going to the bookstore.

"The bookstore?" she said. She was watching TV, sans prostheses, her skirt pulled up on her thighs to expose where her legs ended. She had the window fan blaring and a Ziploc bag full of ice positioned on the back of her neck.

"What do you know about Greek mythology?" I asked her.

"Not much. I mean, Zeus and whatever. Why?"

"She told me her name."

"Who?"

"That girl I talk to."

"Stabbing girl?"

"Well, technically I think she would be *stabbed* girl."

"That's a big step," she said, winking.

"Don't wink."

"I didn't. So what is it?"

"What's what?"

"Her *name*, Louis."

"Frances Hephaestus Jameson."

"She sounds like a weirdo."

"Hephaestus is the Greek god of metalworking. Do you want to go to the bookstore or not?"

"I guess so. Can you push me? Can we get some ice cream?"

"You don't want to walk?"

"I'm tired, Louis. The bookstore is four blocks away. It's hot out. Please push me."

"It's not that hot," I said, but what I meant was it wasn't really that hotter than it always was. It was always boiling downtown. So yeah, it was hot, but I could tell I wasn't going to get her to come with me unless I pushed her. I went to get her wheelchair and put it next to the couch. She transferred herself with all the grace of nine years of practice (not that much grace, actually). Then she smoothed her skirt and pulled her hair up into a ponytail and threw the bag of ice on the coffee table (where my mother would find it later and scream about condensation and wood damage for hours) and gestured toward the front door.

We lived in a nice apartment. There were three big bedrooms and a big living room and a big kitchen and lots of sunlight. We probably wouldn't have been able to afford it now, but my parents had bought it during a housing slump before we were born. They were always planning ahead. Now it was worth about six times what they'd paid for it. The neighborhood had only gotten better over the years. It was, as my father often reminded my mother (because it was his idea), the best investment they'd ever made.

I rolled Willa out the front door and to the elevator. We lived on the sixth floor. There was nothing above us except a garden roof. No swimming pool. We might have been the only midrise in Los Angeles without one, but I didn't like swimming and Willa had resigned herself to a body-of-water-less life. On occasion I could convince her to bob around in an inner tube, but she didn't like getting wet and we were fair, for half-Indian kids, and the water made her sunburn too quickly.

Willa hit the call button for the elevator, and it whirred to life. The building used to have an actual doorman and an actual elevator man, but they'd both been gone for about a decade. I'd never understood the need for elevator help, anyway.

When the door opened, I pushed Willa inside. She had her phone in her lap, so I reached over her and pressed the button for the lobby. I was thinking about Frances, about why she'd decided to reveal her identity now. About how saying it that way made her seem like a superhero. Revealing her identity.

"Aw, she's cute," Willa said.

I leaned over her shoulder and tried to grab her phone away. She was on Frances's Facebook profile, scrolling through her photos.

"Hands off!" she said. "You're the one who told me her name. What did you think I was going to do?"

"Well, you could have asked. I would have showed you."

"I'm showing myself."

She continued to scroll through the photos, pausing on certain ones to zoom in or read the comments.

"Who's this?" she asked, stopping on a photo of Frances and Arrow. The elevator dinged and stopped and the doors opened to the lobby, a 1920s architectural gem (so said both my father and that issue of *Architectural Magazine*).

"Arrow. Her cousin."

"Hmm. She's cute too." She clicked her phone off and slid it into her pocket. "They're both cute. Frances is really cute. I like her."

"I'm glad I have your approval."

"*You* don't have my approval, *she* has my approval. Why did she tell you her name now, anyway? Because her mom died?"

"I guess so. I think she's thinking about doing something. Like finding that movie star I told you about."

"Wallace Green? Because her mom said that's her father?"

"That's what she said."

"Well, fuck. I hope she finds him. Everybody deserves to know who their real parents are. I would freak if Mom or Dad pulled something like that. Family shouldn't lie to family."

There was something in the way she said it. But I was probably being paranoid.

I hadn't told anybody about the University of Texas's offer. But I wasn't *lying*. I was omitting.

Willa pushed the lobby doors open, and I maneuvered the chair out of the building. It was seven o'clock and still boiling and bright out. I headed down Hope Street in the direction of our local bookstore. Mom and Dad made a big deal out of shopping local because they were local, and local business paid the bills.

"What do you need, anyway?" Willa asked. "At the bookstore?"

"I thought I'd get a book on mythology."

"Ohh," Willa said, a truly annoying singsong quality to her voice. "Doesn't this girl live on the other side of the country?"

"*Frances* lives in Maryland, yes. But I'm not reading this book for her."

"You're not reading this book because Hephaestus is the Greek god of metalworking? You just randomly happened to become interested in mythology after Frances told you her name? Didn't I say family doesn't lie to family?"

We were passing in front of Sally's Diner. I still hadn't given Benson his fourteen dollars, but I had the money now. I steered Willa to the entrance.

"Hey!" she said. "What are you doing?"

"I need to give something to Benson. You can wait outside."

"Well, I don't care. I don't care what I do. You can bring me in or I can wait out here, I don't care."

I stopped her chair outside the entrance and then walked around to face her. "Whatever happened to family not lying to family?"

"Oh, ha-ha," she said.

I went inside. Benson brightened, looked behind me, dimmed.

"Here," I said, handing him my debit card. "She's outside. I have to use the bathroom, anyway."

I spent a long time in the bathroom. I pulled my phone out in front of the wall of mirrors and I went to my contacts to find Frances's number. I wanted to text her, to be able to say I had contacted her in another way. Because each new way—TILTgroup, Facebook—seemed important. I wanted to find her in every single possible way. I wanted to invent new profiles in new social media sites so I could contact her in a hundred different ways. All different versions of myself contacting different versions of her. I just wanted her to know—*I am thinking of you.* That's what I would text her.

I am thinking of you.

But she wasn't in my contacts. Hadn't I saved her number?

But I knew I had—I knew I'd saved it. I'd written her number and her address into my phone (*In case you want to mail me something*, she'd wrote, sticking a little smiley face on the end, and I'd read everything over to myself again and again, searching Easton, Maryland, and pulling up maps that showed a town on the water, a small town surrounded by blue). I'd put her into my phone but she wasn't there, and I couldn't help but feel like a tiny part of her was slipping away from me, running through my fingers as I tried to grab on to whatever I could. A small burst of panic even as another voice in my head picked up and told me to relax, you could always find her again. You could always ask her again.

So I opened Facebook and I opened my messages and there was her name, but all the messages were blank. Or else they wouldn't load? But that was where she gave me her phone number, and now I didn't have it. And all the things I lost, they didn't make any sense. I mean, they were as important as Frances's phone number or as unimportant as a matchbox car. There was no rhyme or reason.

I wrote her a message.

I put your number into my phone and now it's gone. I know you'll understand; I know you are the only person who could ever understand. Even though my dad saw it with his own eyes, that doesn't make him understand. I just wanted you to know that I am thinking of you, that I think about you all the time, that I hope you're well. That I wish I could be there tomorrow and I wish I could meet you. I've locked myself in a diner bathroom. I'm pretty sure that guy I told you about really does have a crush on Willa. I'm scared to come out. I wanted to text you but your number is gone. If you give it to me again, I promise I won't lose it. I will write it on my skin in ink.

I sent it before I reread it. She wrote me back quickly.

Be careful: ink stains skin. I'm thinking of you too. I'm thinking of doing something stupid.

She gave me her number again, and I texted her before I could lose my nerve.

Me too.

THIRTEEN

Frances

My mother's wake was closed casket and so I couldn't even really be sure that she was in there. It was a very small ceremony, just Arrow and my grandparents and my aunt and uncle. The six of us. We coupled up. I did not make Arrow wear black. But she insisted on painting her nails a dark, moody purple, and she kept her arm around me as the priest spoke.

Which was funny, really, because none of us were overly religious. My aunt was the only one who went to church. My grandparents could never be bothered and had never so much as asked me if I wanted to go. If I had become curious about it, I'm sure they would have handed me off to Aunt Florence. She knew all the prayers, and she kept a rosary wrapped around her wrists now. It looked more like a pair of handcuffs than a religious symbol.

It did not escape me how perfectly absurd the whole thing was.

It did not escape me that the four adults in my life— grandmother, grandfather, aunt, uncle—had all gotten together five years ago and decided not to tell me my mother had been committed to an insane asylum. I grew up thinking my mother had moved to Florida. I grew up thinking there was a black widow spider that some- times nested in our mailbox. I learned to do without the extravagant wasting of money I had been so accustomed to. I moved into my grandparents' house, and they doted on me appropriately but reservedly. I never wanted for anything.

I wondered if my father—Frances the original—knew my mother was dead. I wondered if he'd read about it in the newspaper. And then I wondered if it had even been in the newspaper, and then I wondered if my father even read the newspaper, and then I wondered if maybe my father wasn't dead too. Who was to say? Nobody had heard from him in years and years and years.

The wake was private, and when it was over we all trudged over to the cemetery and they put my mother's coffin into the ground.

Arrow took my hand. My aunt and my grandmother

held each other and cried. Grandpa Dick and Uncle Irvine stayed to one side.

"Are you okay?" Arrow whispered. We were far enough away from the others that no one could hear us.

"I want to find my father," I said.

"Why, so he can find another office tool to stick into you? No way," she hissed.

"Not him. I mean, I want to find Wallace Green. You'll go with me, right?"

"I already said I would." She paused. "Are you sure you want to do this?"

"Yeah. But, I mean, it's probably not even going to happen. Can you imagine what Grandpa and Grandma are going to say?"

"Are you kidding me? This is the absolute perfect time to ask them. They lied to you for *five years*. They're practically dying for you to ask them for a favor, just so they can say yes."

"I know they're not going to say yes."

"They absolutely are. Twenty bucks."

"Fine," I said. We shook hands.

I knew my grandparents were going to freak out just like I knew I had to do it anyway. Even if we didn't end up meeting Wallace Green, there was something to be said about the physical journey. It was sixteen hundred miles from Maryland to Austin. I wanted to feel each one. I wanted to watch out the window as they slipped away.

I had already made up my mind. I had already practiced the conversation I was going to have with my grandparents. I had already started packing.

I wanted to find Wallace Green.

And I wanted to meet Louis.

We had talked for hours last night.

Well, first we had texted for hours and then he had said:

My fingers are killing me. Can I call you?

And my heart had stopped for a minute and I started panicking a little because he had been so unknown to me for so many years and now he was known, I knew his name, I had seen pictures of him and his sister (who was an absurdly beautiful, unearthly creature with a perpetual scowl on her face), I had texted him on a phone, I knew his phone number. And now he wanted to hear my voice? I have a terrible voice. Grandma Doris always said I talked out of the back of my nose (my grandparents were honest about everything except where my mother had been for the past five years and what kind of arachnids lived in our mailbox).

I was terrified.

But my fingers typed

Yes, call me.

before my brain could stop them.

My fingers had betrayed me.

Or, I don't know, maybe they had done me a favor.

Because Louis had a really, really nice voice.

My phone buzzed in my hands, and I answered it with a *hello* that I hoped wasn't too eager or too uninterested. I was going for the perfect blend of each. The perfect hello.

"Frances? Wow. Frances? This is weird."

I held the phone so tightly in my hand that my fingers hurt. But I didn't care. I only cared about how I could hear him breathe, almost a little out of breath, like maybe he was as nervous as I was. Like maybe his heart was beating just as fast.

"Hi. Louis. This is weird."

"I can't believe I'm finally . . ."

"I know."

"You sound exactly like I thought you'd sound."

"Really? Not too nasally?"

"Not too nasally."

"You sound really nice too. Your voice is deep, but not too deep."

And it was true—he sounded exactly like I thought he would sound, quiet and soft-spoken and a little grumbly and *there*. He was *there*, really, on the other end of the line. We were connected through some series of invisible wavelengths and wires and a satellite beaming us closer. We were closer than we had ever been, and it only made me want more.

"Good. Well, hi. It's nice to talk to you," he said.

"It's nice to talk to you too. Hi."

"Hi."

"Are we going to do this?"

"I think we're going to do this. Right? I think we have to do this."

I'd stayed up too late and now I was tired. My eyes were red and I felt exhausted, like I hadn't slept since my grandparents had pushed a stack of letters at me and told me to start grieving.

A pair of cemetery employees was filling up my mother's grave with dirt. We were supposed to have left by now, but we stayed behind. Just Grandpa and Grandma and me. Aunt Florence and Uncle Irvine had taken Arrow home, against her will, to give us a minute.

"I don't know if I can forgive you," I said.

"We love you more than anybody in the world," Grandma Doris said.

"You shouldn't love me more than Arrow. You should love us equally."

"We do love you equally. Our two granddaughters," Grandma clarified. "But we helped raised you, sweetheart. So forgive us for being a little attached."

"Your mother was a great woman," Grandpa Dick said. He was looking up at the sky, getting teary-eyed in the way that only older men get teary-eyed: with a sense of foreboding and like the end of his life was so imminent and unavoidable.

"Please don't cry," I whispered.

"We wanted you to remember her like a great woman, and not like the sufferer of a terrible disease," he continued.

"That was very poetic," Grandma said. She pulled a handkerchief out of her pocket. I checked, but it wasn't Hank Whitney's. I guess more people than I realized still used handkerchiefs. She dabbed at the corners of her eyes with it and then blew her nose.

"We just thought we had more time. We never would have guessed. . . . It was a tragedy," he added.

"I was old enough to know the truth," I said. "You should have told me the truth."

"One day you'll understand," Grandpa said.

"We'll do anything to make it up to you," Grandma said.

That was the magic phrase. That was what I'd been waiting for.

"I actually have something in mind," I said.

Arrow came over that night. She held her hand out in front of her, unspeaking. I placed a twenty-dollar bill into it.

We left the next day.

FOURTEEN
Louis

"You want to go where? And why?"

My mother was knee-deep in linen. She had bolts of fabric around her, laid out on the floor, one on top of the other like she was building herself a fort.

"Mom, can I help you find something?" I asked.

"The cerulean, Louis. This is sky. This is powder. I can't find the cerulean. Did you sell the rest of the cerulean?"

"No, Mom. I didn't sell any linen."

"And where did you say you wanted to go? Anaheim? Like Disneyland?"

"Austin. I want to go to Austin."

"Austin? Like Texas? What's in Texas?"

"Can you stop moving around for a minute? You're making me nervous."

"I'm making you nervous? How about I'm making myself nervous because I can't find the cerulean." She paused, put her hands on her hips. Glared at me. "Wait a minute. Did you have the cerulean last?"

"I didn't have the cerulean."

"Because you know you have a tendency to—"

"I didn't have it! I haven't seen it. Mom, lemme talk to you for a minute."

"Fine, Louis. What do you want? You want to go to Texas?"

"Yeah, Austin. I want to go to Austin."

"Okay, what's in Austin?"

I couldn't tell her the truth (which was that Frannie and I had talked for hours on the phone and decided that yes—we were both going to do it. She was going to find Wallace Green and I was going to tour the University of Texas and decide whether I wanted to spend four years of my life playing tennis for them) so I'd spent the morning coming up with the perfect lie. If I said I was going to a tennis tournament, she'd do some research. She and my father both loved being involved in my tennis career. They'd want to know who I was playing, where I was playing. Everything.

"A music festival," I said.

My parents didn't care about any music that had been produced after the 1970s, so that was the perfect answer.

"You want to go all the way to Texas to see a concert?" she asked.

"Well, it's a music festival, Mom. It's a lot of concerts."

"Like Woodstock?"

"I guess kind of like Woodstock. Except less drugs. Is that okay? I mean, I know it's short notice."

"When is it?"

"I was kind of hoping to leave tomorrow?"

"Tomorrow as in the day after today?"

"Yeah, I was hoping."

She sat down on a wobbling tower of fabric. "That's short notice, Louis."

"I know, Mom. I wasn't expecting to get tickets. It was kind of a sudden thing."

"Are you going by yourself?"

"I'm going to take Zach."

"I don't love Zach," she said. She ran her hands through her hair. She looked tired.

"Zach's fine."

She narrowed her eyes at me. "Louis. Is everything okay? Are you in some kind of trouble?"

"No! Everything's fine. It's just a music festival, Mom."

"You're a terrible liar, Louis."

"I'm not lying," I said, but I'd lost what little steam I'd

had to begin with; it didn't even sound convincing to me.

I waited for some kind of reaction. She looked tired. She spun around in a slow circle, still looking for the missing ream of cerulean linen. Finally she straightened up and looked at me.

"You're supposed to work at the store."

"It will only be a few days. I could get Willa to cover my shifts."

"I don't like the idea of this. Texas is so far away."

"I'll be safe. I'll text you all the time."

"A music festival?" she asked. "With Zach?"

"He's responsible. We're both responsible!"

"There's no music festival, is there? You've always been such a terrible liar. Are you sure you're not in trouble?"

"I'm not in trouble, I promise."

She was quiet for a long time. I could practically feel her going back and forth, trying to balance the fact that I was an adult with the fact that she was overprotective, one of many by-products of my sister's accident.

"I know you should be able to make your own decisions. I know it's your car, and you have your own money."

"So I can go?"

"You can go," she said, exhaling. "But you're not taking Zach. You're taking Willa."

"Willa? I can't take Willa."

"Why not?"

"Because she . . ."

Because she was legless? Because she had never been away from home without my parents before? Because if I put her wheelchair in my trunk, where would the suitcases go? Because I was terrified she was going to find out I was thinking of leaving?

"Because you're taking your sister or you're not going."

"What if she doesn't want to go?"

"She'll want to go. Now don't make me regret whatever this is. Okay? Let me go, I need to find that cerulean."

She wouldn't find it.

I had lied to her.

I had put it into the trunk of my car at my father's request. I'd taken it to a client's. Gave them what they wanted. Put the remaining fabric in my trunk and brought it back to the store.

The trunk was still warm where it had once been.

"This might not interest you at all," I said to Willa later.

She was on our roof deck with a pair of binoculars. I didn't ask questions.

"What might not interest me at all?" she said.

"I'm driving to Austin tomorrow."

"Like, Texas?" she asked, lowering the binoculars. "What's in Texas?"

"A music festival," I said.

"What music festival?"

"Austin City Limits."

"Huh. I think I've heard of it. Is Zach going with you? Isn't that who you usually do nerdy things with?"

"Zach can't go," I said. "And music isn't nerdy."

Zach also played tennis in the Pacific Palisades. We were friends because it was easy and we got along fine and we both liked music. And tennis, obviously. (I was better.)

"Huh," she repeated.

"I mean, you probably don't want to go, and I get it. I just thought I'd offer."

"I'll go," she said, shrugging. "I've never been to Texas. I've never been on a road trip either. Ugh—am I lame? It feels like I'm lame. When did you say you're leaving?"

"Tomorrow."

"Tomorrow? We're both supposed to work at the store."

"Mom said we could go. You don't have to, if you don't want to."

"Do you not want me to go? It feels like you're inviting me to go but you don't want me to go. Wait—did Mom make you ask me?"

"I want you to go. I mean, if you want."

"It all seems rather suspicious," she said. She turned her chair around. I wondered why she wasn't wearing her legs.

"There's nothing suspicious about it, weirdo."

"I beg to differ. But if I keep your secrets for you, you

have to keep mine. And that might be valuable in the future. So yes, I'll go to Austin with you."

"I don't have any secrets. You know, maybe we stopped your therapy too early? You seem a little unstable."

"Well, unless the city of Austin has decided to do you a huge, personal favor and move ACL from October to June—which I guess we can't rule out, because you're so important and influential in the music community—you're lying to Mom and Dad about why you're going to Texas. And Mom knows you're lying, because everybody knows when you're lying, because you're a truly abysmal liar. And that's why she's making you bring me. Because I am more responsible than you, and so whatever drug trade you're getting yourself into, I might be able to save you when you are swiftly arrested from some nameless border town."

"I think you have a very healthy, active imagination," I said.

"Do I? Or do I just happen to know ACL isn't anytime soon? So you're fucking busted, and you owe me one."

"I'm really that bad of a liar?"

"Literally the worst. Like you should never do anything remotely devious because it will be written all over your face."

"What secrets do you need me to keep for you, anyway?"

"In time," she said. "Everything will reveal itself in time."

"Well that isn't cryptic at all," I said. But she'd turned away from me again. She'd raised the binoculars to her eyes. She didn't listen to me anymore.

I texted Frannie:

Everything is falling into place.

FIFTEEN
Frances

Grandma Doris woke up at five in the morning and started baking. When I came down to the kitchen at eight, the kitchen counters were covered in loaves of bread. She was still wearing black. She was a very traditional mourner.

"Morning," I said. (I only got the pun after I'd said it.)

"Morning, Frances. I'm making bread."

"I see that. What are you making bread for?"

"For your trip, honey. Bread will keep well. I have some zucchini bread and some sprouted wheat bread and some banana nut bread."

"You didn't have to do all this."

"I couldn't sleep."

"Well, thanks," I said. "Everything looks great."

She removed her apron and draped it over a kitchen chair, then turned to me and leaned against the counter. "I never really thought it was a possibility that one of my daughters might go before me," she said quietly. "You have kids, you know, you just take it for granted that they're going to outlive you. That's the way it's supposed to be."

"Grandma," I said, feeling my voice start to crack. My grandmother had always been such a pillar of strength, an old-fashioned society lady with never a hair out of place or a lipstick line smudged, and here she was, looking flawless in the morning even with flour on the tips of her fingers. But I could see her edges wavering. I could tell she was starting to lose it. "I'm sorry," I added. It was the only thing I could think to say.

"Do you remember my friend Dana? When her husband died, she sat shiva for him. Seven days, she didn't leave the house. I brought her bread. She told me, 'I don't know what I would do without this.' Other people, they lose the ones they love and they have to get over it. Go back to work! Stop crying! But here, this is something more. This is time, Frannie. I just want time. It makes me wish we were religious—the idea of sitting shiva is very appealing to me."

"You can still sit shiva if you want to," I said.

"Do you think so? But are you allowed to bake during

shiva, Frannie? I wanted to bake. I wouldn't know how to do it."

"You can do whatever you want. Sit shiva or don't. Bake or don't."

"You don't think that's hypocritical?" she asked. "Picking and choosing like that?"

"I think a lot of people do that. I think you can do whatever you need to do, whatever helps."

"Do you believe in God, Frances? Or—a god. I don't think I've ever asked you."

"I don't think so," I said.

"How come?"

"I don't have a profound answer."

"I think everything you say is profound," she said, and winked.

I realized then that I forgave her, that I'd been waiting to forgive her because I hated being mad at her, and because I was glad they had lied to me. I think it felt better to have lived the last five years of my life thinking my mother was in Florida than it would have been thinking my mother was insane.

"When are you leaving?" she asked.

"I won't be gone long. You don't have to be sad."

"I'm not sad at all. You're almost a grown-up now. You want to drive sixteen hundred miles away from here? Okeydokey."

"You're gonna miss me."

"I'm going to be busy sitting shiva," she said.

"I'll call you every day. I'll be back in a week and half. You'll be fine."

"Oh, Frances. I'm so honored to know you."

"Geez, Grandma, can you stop acting like I'm never going to see you again?" I crossed the kitchen and hugged her. She smelled like baking soda and yeast. "Thanks for all the bread."

"Well, it was the least I could do."

"Your least is greater than most people's most," I said.

It took her a minute to work out, but when I pulled away, she was smiling.

The first month I spent in my grandparents' house, I was a monster.

I threw tantrums that lasted hours. I painted on the walls with lipstick. I put the stopper in the tub and let the water overflow. I ran away three times.

Finally, my grandfather installed a lock on my bedroom door.

"This is for your own good," he said.

I pretended to be a prisoner in a castle.

They locked me in at night. I wasn't sleeping back then. I composed letters to my mother. I drew stamps on the envelopes and threw them out my bedroom window (which my grandfather had rigged so it only opened an inch. They were scared I would jump out and break a leg in a foolhardy escape attempt). In the morning, Grandpa Dick collected them. I watched from the window and if he happened to look up at me I stuck my tongue out at him.

I wanted to see my cousin.

Arrow and I had always been close. Best friends since Aunt Florence and Uncle Irvine had flown to Vietnam to pick her up from the orphanage that had been her home since birth.

For the longest time, she had rattled on in baby-talk Vietnamese. We communicated in a kind of secret language, a mixture of words from both our languages.

Grandpa Dick said I couldn't see Arrow until I promised to stop running away. So I promised. And he said, "I mean, you have to promise it and mean it."

"I do mean it!"

"I know you're lying, Frances, and it makes me uncomfortable. I'm very uncomfortable with liars." (So said the man of the eventual black-widow-spider-in-the-mailbox yarn.)

"I'm not lying! I'm not going to run away!"

I was lying.

I had researched how many Peter Pan buses it would take me to get to Florida (surprisingly, only three) and I knew exactly how much cash I'd need to cover the fare and food until I reached my mother's house (three hundred). I did not know where my mother's house was, exactly, nor did I know where I was going to get the three hundred dollars, but I was working on the details.

"I know you're lying. When you stop lying, you can see Arrow again."

My bedroom window faced Arrow's bedroom window. We didn't have cell phones yet, so we communicated at night by flicking a flashlight on and off. Mine was a heavy black thing that I'd taken a bright-pink permanent marker to: *Frannie*. We invented our own sort of Morse code, except I'm not sure either of us knew what the other was talking about. Then I lost my flashlight and we were forced to communicate during the day, by writing messages on construction paper. But the messages had to be pretty big in order for us to read them, so we couldn't fit too many words on the paper. Usually we said things like:

Hi.

Sad.

Miss u.

Me too.

Ugh sucks.

OK bye.

It wasn't the most effective means of communication, but it was our only present option.

Weeks went by. Every day my grandfather asked me the same thing:

"If I leave this door unlocked tonight, are you going to try to run away?"

Every day I had the same reply:

"No."

When he finally believed me, it felt like a religious miracle. He stopped locking my bedroom door at night, and he let Arrow come over whenever she wanted.

"Are you gonna run away, though?" she asked.

"Eventually, yeah," I said.

I was lying.

Arrow came over lugging two suitcases. Aunt Florence and Uncle Irvine trailed behind her with Tupperware containers full of cookies and peanut butter and jelly sandwiches and *thit kho*, a Vietnamese dish Aunt Florence made once a month because it had always been Arrow's favorite. The six of us loaded up the back of my 1993 Volvo 240 classic (named Kathy) and then stood on the front lawn in a misshapen circle.

"What an experience," Aunt Florence said. She didn't really look like my mom except they had the same hair and the same hands, hands that always had to be doing something. Right now she was fussing around with Arrow's pinned-on lace collar. Arrow was slapping her away.

"I've never been to Texas myself," Uncle Irvine said, and then he waited like he maybe wanted us to invite him.

"Never let her drop below a quarter tank," Grandpa Dick advised, putting his hand on Kathy's hood. "You never know where the next gas station will be."

Actually I had an app that listed the ten closest gas stations, but I didn't tell him this, because he didn't know what apps were.

"Call us once a day. No exceptions. You skip a day, I call the police and file a missing persons report. Got it?" Grandma said.

"Grandma, relax," Arrow said. "I lived by myself in Vietnam for *three years*. I'll be fine in Texas."

"You know this is different than that, Arrow," Aunt Florence said, rolling her eyes.

"The orphanage was understaffed. I used to go get sticky rice by myself. I'd be gone for hours," Arrow said. "I'm just saying. Frannie and I will be fine. We both have Mace."

"Mace is illegal. You have Mace?" Grandpa Dick said.

"It isn't illegal," I said.

"It's illegal if you're under eighteen. Why do you need Mace, anyway? I showed you those self-defense moves."

"Arrow weighs ninety-five pounds," I said. "Who is she going to defend herself against? An eight-year-old?"

"Offended," Arrow said. "Timothy Banks is really big for an eight-year-old."

"You used Mace on an eight-year-old?" Uncle Irvine said.

"No, she karate-chopped him in the neck," I explained. "He was fine. We have to go. I don't think Grandma is even supposed to be outside."

"Why is Grandma not supposed to be outside?" Aunt Florence asked.

"She's sitting shiva," I said.

"Mom? We're not Jewish."

"I liked the idea," Grandma said. "You can bring over some casseroles."

"I think that sounds like a great idea," Uncle Irvine said. "Doris, I would love to sit shiva with you."

"Honey, shiva lasts a week," Aunt Florence whispered.

"I would love to sit shiva with you for this afternoon," Uncle Irvine amended.

"All are welcome," Grandma said, shrugging.

Arrow and I got into the car, leaving them to discuss the specifics of shiva and what kinds of casserole Grandma was partial to.

I was driving the first shift. Arrow settled back in her seat and put her feet up on the dashboard.

"I guess we're kind of sitting shiva too," she said. "I mean, in a way. Like, we're sitting. And we're both in mourning."

I felt like I'd been sitting shiva my whole life. First my father. Then my mother. And then, because the universe worked in strange ways, my mother again.

"A mobile shiva," I said.

"You know, we have a kind of shiva too," Arrow said. "In Vietnamese culture, the wake can last five or six days."

"What do they do?"

"They mourn. They put coins in the dead person's mouth."

"Coins? Why?"

"I don't know. They don't really need them anymore, right?"

I didn't answer. I imagined my mother with coins in her mouth. Then I imagined my mother buried. Then I imaged my mother alive and living in an over-fifty-five gated community in Florida. I preferred the latter.

That is how I chose to remember her.

SIXTEEN
Louis

Willa and I left early the next morning. My father was still in Dubai; he sent his blessings via text message. My mother gave us three hundred dollars for food and reminded us how lucky we were that she was letting us leave during the store's busiest month.

"Ma, I help with the books," Willa said. "June is not our busiest month. And we're only going to be gone for a few days. Like a week, tops."

"One of the busiest months, whatever," Mom replied, waving her hands.

We got in the car a little after nine o'clock. Willa had overslept.

"I have to stop somewhere first," she said.

"Where?"

"The diner. I want some breakfast."

"You want some breakfast or you want to say good-bye to Benson?"

"It just so happens that I am able to, as they say, kill two birds with one stone," Willa said.

"What's the deal with you two, anyway? He obviously has a crush on you, and as far as I can see, you're kind of leading him on."

"We're eighteen, Louis, I don't think we have crushes anymore."

"So he has deep, romantic feelings for you?"

"Look, if you're going to be a dick about it—"

"I'm not. I'm sorry. What . . . Do you like him? I mean, do you like each other? Are you dating?"

"Can you calm down?" Willa asked. "Not everything has to be so neatly explained. He's a person who's staying in Los Angeles. I am a person who is temporarily leaving Los Angeles. I am going to say good-bye to him. Okay?"

"I'm not saying good-bye to anyone."

"You don't really have any friends."

"Hey."

"Sorry. You don't."

"I have Zach."

"You just play tennis with Zach. And sometimes you go see concerts. You've never even had him over for dinner."

"Guys don't have other guys over for dinner."

"You could if you wanted to. But you don't. Because you're scared he's a little better at tennis than you."

"Zach's not better at tennis than me!"

"He could be. He just doesn't care enough. You care a lot. Maybe that's why you don't have any friends."

I pulled into the diner parking lot and inched my way into a space. "I have Frances."

"You don't have Frances. You've never even met her," she said.

"What is this fucking attack, Willa? We're not even out of town yet."

I turned the car off and looked at her. She was suddenly pale; she had her dress pulled up and she was playing with the top of her right prosthetic, where fake met real. I reached over and took her hand.

"Hey. Does it hurt?"

"No," she said quietly. Then, with some difficulty: "I'm sorry I'm being a bitch."

"Accepted. Is there a reason?"

"No. I don't know. I'm not nervous or anything, if that's what you're going to say. Do you want to come in?"

"Do you want a minute?"

"No. Come in, please. Can you come around? I need an arm."

I got out of the car and walked around to the passenger's side. Willa opened her door and pulled herself out of the car. She gripped my arm firmly, and we made our way across the parking lot.

"I could get the chair?" I offered.

"I'm just a little tired," she said.

"I could run to the medical supply store and get you a walker?"

She elbowed me in the ribs but laughed.

Benson wasn't at the host's stand. Instead it was his older brother, Thad. Thad was a very stereotypical surfer. I only ever saw him wear a shirt when he did shifts at the diner, and it was always the same shirt: blue with three surfboards leaning against a wooden fence. I think it was the only one he had and I couldn't tell if he wore it ironically or not.

"Hey, twins," he said. "Table for *dos*?"

"Just takeout, actually," I said.

"Is Benson not here?" Willa asked.

"Sick day for the little bro," Thad said, shrugging. "I think he consumed some gnarly egg rolls." (He actually said gnarly, which is something nobody in real life says except Thad, who says it often.) "I'll tell him you send your well wishes."

"Thanks," Willa said. I ordered for both of us, and we waited in plastic chairs by the door.

"Sorry," I said.

"It's whatever."

"We can swing by his apartment?"

"Really not necessary."

"I mean, I know how upset I'd be if I didn't get to say good-bye to Zach."

"You're funny," she said, smiling.

"You know how you said I haven't met Frances yet?"

"Yeah."

"Well, I'm going to meet Frances."

"What? Wait—is that what this trip is about? You're driving halfway across the country to meet a girl?"

"No, actually. Although I don't think there would be anything wrong with that."

"Well, it would mean *she* was driving halfway across the country to meet *you*," Willa said. "And there would be something wrong with that—poor girl."

"Neither of us is driving to Austin to meet each other. It's just a very unique coincidence."

"Why is she going there? Oh, wait! Is this about Wallace Green?"

"She is going there to try to find Wallace Green, yes."

"Insane. Okay, Frances is insane. Noted. And why are *you* going there?"

I didn't want to tell her, but it hadn't escaped me that we'd eventually show up on the doorstep of the University of Texas for a prearranged private tour. Willa was pretty smart; she was bound to suspect something at that point. I might as well let her in on the secret now.

"Okay. Listen. I haven't told anyone."

"Oh my gosh, it's really drugs."

"What?"

"You're involved in an international drug cartel."

"I can't tell if you're joking. But no."

"Oh, good. I didn't bring my running legs."

"Funny. This is actually . . . not the easiest for me to say. But I have some kind of big news."

I had Willa's full attention now, which didn't happen all that often. I was about to tell her about the scholarship when Thad yelled my name and held up our bag of food. I went over to pay and pick it up. Willa held the door open for me.

"You are very good at building suspense," she said in the car.

"I don't mean to. I'm just trying to find the right words. Okay. I got offered a full ride to the University of Texas."

I thought Willa might scream, but instead she dropped the tater tot she was holding and stared at me. I could feel her staring at me, but I was merging onto the highway so I couldn't look over at her. This time of day there was no traffic going east, so once we were on the highway, I returned her stare. I didn't know what that stare meant. It either meant she was happy for me or she wanted to kill me. With Willa, it was hard to tell, and sometimes it could be both at the same time.

Finally, in a small voice, she said, "You're already applying for schools? We're not even seniors yet."

"I didn't apply. They came and saw me play. I guess

they must have requested my transcript. I got the letter a couple days ago—it's more like a placeholder kind of thing. If I decide to apply for next year, I'm guaranteed a spot as long as my grades stay up. Could you grab my sunglasses? They're in the glove compartment."

Willa wrenched open the glove compartment and dug around. "There are no sunglasses in here."

"I just put them there this morning. They're in there."

"They're not here, Louis. You got the letter *a couple days ago* and you're just telling me now?"

"Could you look again? I know I put them—"

"THEY ARE NOT IN HERE, LOUIS," she yelled. Okay, she was yelling. This was better than the quiet, even tone of before. "YOU GOT THE LETTER A COUPLE DAYS AGO AND YOU'RE JUST TELLING ME NOW?"

"I needed some time to think about it! I wasn't going to tell everyone if I ended up not even being interested."

"I'm not *everyone*," she said. Quiet and even again. "I'm your sister. I'm your twin. I'm your best friend."

"I thought you said I didn't have any friends."

"And you decided to wait a couple days to tell me. . . . Well, fine. That's just fine. Congratulations, though. It's a huge accomplishment and even if you don't decide to go, I know you've worked harder at tennis than anything else in your entire life. It must feel pretty good that it's all paid off."

"That was surprisingly sincere."

"Because I *am* sincere, you asshat. I'm happy for you. Also, fine. I'm being a little hypocritical. I haven't told you everything either."

"What haven't you told me? About Benson? Are you guys in love or something?"

It was a joke, but it was also the wrong joke, except I didn't know it was the wrong joke until I heard Willa sigh and saw her wipe at her face angrily. I looked over at my sister, and she was as close to tears as I had ever seen her. Her eyes were wet.

"Willa?"

"Here's the really short version, okay?" she said. "Benson and I have been dating for . . . a while. That is why it is hypocritical of me to be mad at you right now. But I'm still mad."

"How long is a while?"

"We dated all through junior year. And then we . . . I broke it off. A couple weeks ago. And he's trying to get me back, I guess."

"What? You dated for an entire year? And you didn't tell anyone?"

"I mean, I told Stacy. Benson told a couple of his friends, I guess. But I didn't want it to be public knowledge because . . . I don't know. It was my first real relationship. And I didn't want Mom to know and I didn't want you—I mean, anyone. I just didn't want anyone to know."

"Okay. So why did you break it off?"

"Because he wants to, like . . . Ugh, this is weird. You're my brother. He wants to take our relationship . . . Gross. Use your imagination."

"Willa, is he pressuring you to—"

"No! No. Gosh, don't be so melodramatic. We've just talked about it a lot. And I don't think I'm ready."

"But if you like him, you don't have to—"

"I don't think I'll ever be ready, okay, Louis? I don't think I'll ever be ready to be, like . . . I mean, I don't have any legs, okay? I don't have any legs."

Willa reached into the bag and pulled out one of the breakfast sandwiches. She handed it to me, and I understood that to mean she didn't want me to say anything.

The next few hours of the ride were spent in silence.

The miles ticked away. The road opened ahead of us.

We were quiet.

PART TWO

Found

SEVENTEEN
Frances

We spent the night in one of those terrible, cheap, nameless motels. Arrow brought a sleeping bag big enough for two, and she laid it down on top of the comforter and for a minute I didn't know what she was doing. But then she withdrew two pillows from a suitcase (the suitcase contained only the two pillows and sat empty upon their removal), and she placed the pillows at the top of the sleeping bag, arranging them so they weren't touching any part of the comforter.

"Arrow?" I said. "The blankets are included in our $39.99."

"When Mom and Dad brought me home from the

orphanage, I had lice," Arrow said. "I know what kind of shit is living in these communal blankets."

I had never actually stayed in a motel before, so I deferred to Arrow's expertise.

Arrow and I had made it to a place called Blountville, Tennessee, which was an hour and a half outside Knoxville and a solid seven hours' drive from Easton. Except it hadn't taken us seven hours, it had taken us nine hours, because Arrow made us stop to pee every hour and fifteen minutes. And she couldn't eat while she drove. And even if she didn't need to pee, she insisted on stretching her legs and feeling the sunshine on her face.

"The car has windows," I told her. "You can feel the sunshine while we drive."

"It's not the same."

She turned the TV on in the motel room but kept the volume muted. We sat on top of the sleeping bag with our legs crossed and our pajamas on. Arrow wore pink, fuzzy slippers. I called my grandparents.

"Hello?" Grandpa Dick answered.

"Hi, Grandpa."

"Frannie! Or Arrow? I don't know, you both sound the same. Where are you?"

"Frannie. We're in Tennessee, Grandpa!"

"Ah, Tennessee. They're in Tennessee, Doris. Whereabouts?"

"Blountville."

"Never heard of it."

I could hear my grandmother in the background, instructing him on what to say.

"Why don't you give Grandma the phone?" I said. "She's being loud."

There was a scuffle as the phone exchanged hands. My grandmother breathed heavily into the receiver. "Frannie? Or Arrow?"

"Frannie," I said. "Hi, Grandma. How are you?"

"Oh, doing fine, dear. Sitting shiva, playing a lot of card games. It's been very nice. I feel like I haven't had a chance to just sit and think for so long. And it feels good to dedicate this time to your mother. To her memory. It feels important."

"I'm glad you're doing okay, Grandma."

"What about you? How was your first day on the road?"

"It was okay. Arrow pees a lot."

"Tell her I said hi, dear."

"Grandma says hi," I told Arrow.

"Hi, Grandma," Arrow said.

"She says hi," I said into the receiver.

"Are you stopped for the night?" Grandma asked.

"Yeah, we're in a motel in Tennessee. Arrow has disinfected everything, and I think we're going to turn in soon."

"Arrow's always been weird about germs," Grandma said thoughtfully. "Is everything else okay?"

"Everything's fine."

"The car is okay?"

"The car's okay."

"You're eating enough?"

"Yes."

"Did you have some of the bread?"

"The banana bread. It was really good."

"The trick is you have to use old bananas. Not rotten, you know, but just on the cusp. And I like to add walnuts."

"The walnuts were good."

"Well, I won't keep you anymore, Frannie. I'm glad you're safe. Tell Arrow to go easy on the Lysol. I love you both."

"Love you too, Grandma," I said. I hung up and tossed my phone on the mattress.

"How's Grandma?" Arrow asked.

"She's still sitting shiva."

"She wouldn't be sitting shiva if she knew you were really driving to Austin to meet a boy," Arrow said.

When I'd told Arrow we were meeting Louis and his sister in Austin, I tried to make it clear that it wasn't my main incentive for going. It was a happy coincidence that the universe had offered up. I was simply taking advantage of it.

"As long as he doesn't take advantage of you," Arrow had said, narrowing her eyes and turning her attention back to her half-packed suitcase.

She had trust issues. It came, she said, from spending the

first three years of her life in an orphanage. Lice wasn't the only thing she came to America with; she'd also developed a fairly problematic attachment phobia.

"You're not going to tell her, and I'm not going to tell her, so she won't have anything to worry about," I said.

"I'm still skeptical about this," she said. "Let it be known."

"Trust me, it's known. But Louis is sweet. I've known him for a really long time."

"Yes, but you've only known his name for about three days. I'm not convinced he isn't a serial killer."

"Well, if you think I don't actually know him because we haven't met in real life, then you must also believe I am only at a twenty-five percent risk of being murdered by him," I said. I didn't let her respond. I went into the bathroom and shut the door.

"You better disinfect that toilet seat!" she yelled at me.

She'd left the bottle of Lysol on the counter. I sprayed the toilet seat (I wasn't nearly as germ crazy as she was, but I also wasn't about to look a bottle of Lysol in the mouth) and wiped it down with a roll of paper towels she'd also left in there.

I peed and washed my hands, then brushed my teeth and washed my face. Arrow had left a clean towel hanging out of one of the drawers so I grabbed it to dry off. The drawer came ajar a little and when I put the towel back, I saw something catch the light from inside. I pulled open the drawer, which was bare except for a pair of black sunglasses.

I pulled them out and put them on without thinking.

They were too big for my face and kept sliding down the bridge of my nose. I opened the bathroom door, and Arrow recoiled in fear.

"WHAT THE HELL ARE THOSE?" she squealed, pointing at my face.

"I found them!" I said.

She catapulted herself across the room and ripped them from my face. She threw them in the bathroom sink and murdered them with Lysol. I watched the tiny, iridescent bubbles cling to the polarized lenses.

"Are you *insane*?" she asked. "You're going to get pink eye. And I was in the middle of my nightly meditations. I have to start over now. This is disgusting."

"I thought they looked kind of cool."

"You're probably going to get eye cancer now, and that is *not* cool."

Arrow stomped back over to the bed. She had turned the TV off. She folded her legs carefully underneath her and resumed her meditation pose.

I ran the sunglasses under water and dried them off with a paper towel. When I put them back on, they were cool and smelled of disinfectant. I got my phone and took a picture in the mirror. I sent it to Louis.

He wrote back a few seconds later.

Where did you find those?

In my hotel! Cool, huh? Arrow cleaned them,
don't worry.

What brand are they??

I checked the tiny name on the side and wrote back:

Maui Jim. Why?

No freaking way.

What?

Check the left lens. Is it chipped? Like a
huge gouge near the top?

I turned the sunglasses over in my hands, and just like
he said, there was a huge chip in one of the lenses.

How did you know that?

I texted him back:

They are? They're chipped?

> Yeah, where you said they'd be.

> I swear, those are my sunglasses. I swear. I
> just lost them today.

I put the sunglasses on the bathroom counter and looked at them, suddenly terrified, like they might do something. Louis had said, just a few days ago: *Do you ever feel like everything disappears?*

I wrote back with numb, unsure fingers:

> What does this mean? How did these get
> here?

> I have no idea

Then he typed for a long time while I watched the screen and momentarily forgot how to breathe. He finally sent:

> These things . . . It feels like we've found
> a way to cut a hole in the air and walk
> through an opening into a portal that leads
> someplace else. Like there are tears in
> reality and the things we lose aren't lost but
> transported to another world.

Well, this bathroom wasn't another world, but it might as well be. Los Angeles to Tennessee. It wasn't as far as you could get, but it also wasn't immediately explainable how Louis's sunglasses had ended up in my motel bathroom.

I wrote him back.

> Are you sure?

> So sure. Those are my freaking sunglasses.
> I don't even know.

> Well, I'll bring them to you.

I put my phone down next to the sunglasses.

I stared at each inanimate object in turn, like one of them might do something interesting. Like one of them might disappear.

Neither moved.

I went to bed.

And when I woke up, they were still there.

EIGHTEEN
Louis

Los Angeles faded away into the distance and was replaced by nothing. Just the road in front of us and desert surrounding us. I drove for seven or eight hours. I wished my car had hand controls so Willa and I could switch on and off. I wished I had remembered to get a shot of Freon (I had looked up what it was), because even with the air conditioning blasting it was still too hot. Willa leaned forward and put her forehead against the vent.

"I think we have to stop soon, Louis," she said. "I'm sitting in a pool of my own sweat."

"Noted," I said.

"And I have to pee. And I feel like it's been fifteen hours since we ate lunch."

"It's been six," I said.

It was seven p.m. now, and I wasn't eager to stop. There was something to be said about driving through the night, something strangely appealing about the stamina that would require.

Then again, there wasn't much appealing about falling asleep at the wheel.

I got off at the next exit.

Willa vetoed two motels before we found one that met whatever expectations she had set. There was a diner across the street; we headed over after we checked into our room. The hostess gave Willa a long, not unkind look. I realized it had been a while since I'd seen someone stare at my sister's legs. Everyone knew us back home. Nobody was that thrown by them anymore.

"Chill," Willa said when we were seated. She opened the menu. It was enormous; it covered her entire body.

"What?"

"I said you need to chill. You can't let that shit bother you."

"It's rude."

"Look, it's human nature. It's the same reason you do a double take when you see someone with purple hair. We're drawn to the different. She can't help herself. And if it doesn't bother me, it shouldn't bother you."

"How can you be so confident with random strangers but so weird with . . ."

Willa looked at me over the top of her menu. "Are you going to finish that sentence?"

"Maybe later."

"Good decision. I'm ready to order. You think they serve breakfast all day? They must, right? All diners do. I'm going to get some tater tots."

The server came over and Willa ordered first, rambling off a bunch of sides and expressing her sincere gratitude that they did, in fact, serve breakfast all day. When it was my turn, I asked for a salad. I was suddenly not very hungry.

"Do you feel okay?" Willa asked. "Because you just ordered the lamest thing on the menu, and that concerns me."

"Just tired," I said.

To be honest, I didn't really know what I was. I was tired, but not overly so. I was nervous to meet Frances and tour the university, but not overly so. And I was irritated that the hostess had spent so long looking at my sister. I was irritated at the way her eyes had traveled up and down Willa's body, pausing where my sister's real legs met her fake legs.

I didn't know why it bothered me so much. And I didn't know why I was suddenly itchy—like my skin had been dunked in a barrel of chili powder. My throat felt closed up and small.

"Louis?" Willa said.

"I think I'm going to head back to the room," I said quickly, standing up before she could say anything. "Grab mine to go, will you?"

I heard her call after me, but I didn't turn around.

There was no warning.

This was how it happened. There was never any warning.

I just didn't know why it was happening now, after I'd been so good for so long. I had learned to manage my panic attacks by counting (as Willa had obviously noticed). I tried to run through some numbers in my head, but I was already too far gone for it to do anything.

I ran from the diner to the motel. It was one of those motels that are laid out in a strip. Our room was around the back and faced a large, empty parking lot. At the other end of the parking lot was a movie theater that looked like it had been abandoned for at least twenty years. It was covered in green vines, and a large section of it had crumbled in on itself. There was yellow caution tape around the debris but they hadn't gotten around to cleaning it up yet.

Something about it was depressing; I closed the blinds and locked the door behind me.

I sat down on the bed and focused on my breathing. I counted in and I counted out, trying to make my breaths come evenly. My skin burned but at the same time felt somehow detached from my body. It felt like something that did not belong to me, like something I had stolen. It felt like I would split open if I didn't release the pressure that was building underneath it.

I wanted to.

But I couldn't.

I hadn't purposefully cut my skin in years and I didn't want tonight to be the night it came back, in this mostly shitty hotel room while my sister asked for my salad in a Styrofoam to-go container at an equally shitty diner across the street. I didn't want that to be how I spent my first night on the road, my first night away from home. I didn't want "being someone who cut his skin" to be what defined me anymore.

I got off the bed and walked back and forth across the small room, counting my steps until I fell into a rhythm I didn't have to concentrate on anymore. I tried to reclaim my skin, like Dr. Williams told me I had to do, to convince my mind that it was okay and it was supposed to be here and there was nothing wrong with it.

I counted, counted.

And when I got to one hundred, I realized my skin wasn't crawling anymore.

That was nice.

I took a shower and brushed my teeth with a towel around my waist. I heard a key turning in the lock and then the door opened and the lights went out suddenly. I saw a beam of light shine across the room. I poked my head out of the bathroom.

"Willa?"

She held the flashlight under her chin and grinned broadly. "Where'd you get this?" she asked.

"That's not mine."

"It was right outside the door. You must have left it there."

"I think I'd remember if I did."

"I guess someone left it," she said, shrugging. "Got your salad," she said, handing me the container. She turned the lights back on and tossed the flashlight on one of the beds and I picked it up, curious.

It was enormous and black and heavy, clearly very old and made out of some type of metal. I turned it over in my palms and saw the writing—faded with time but still pink and still readable: *Frannie*.

"Are you feeling better? What was wrong, anyway?" Willa asked.

"I'm fine. Where did you say you found this?"

"It was just outside the door, why?"

"Look," I said, pushing it toward her. I put the salad on one of the bureaus and waited while she read the word on the flashlight a few times, her lips moving slightly.

"Is this a joke?" she said.

"It's not a joke. I've never seen this before."

"But why does it say Frannie?"

"I think it says Frannie because it belongs to Frannie."

"I'm worried about your brain," she said.

"I think you should worry about the universe breaking."

"You don't actually think this is hers? And it just, what? Magically appeared outside our motel room?"

"That's kind of exactly what I think happened."

I could tell she wasn't going to believe me. Willa wasn't really open-minded when it came to stuff like this. She might not think I was a fabric drug dealer, like my mother, but I knew she also didn't believe the things I lost were anything other than just that: lost. I decided not to press the issue.

"You know, I think this is a sign," she said, flicking the lights on and holding up the flashlight thoughtfully.

"The flashlight is a sign?"

"When was the last time you did something you weren't supposed to? I mean, besides lying to me about college."

"I don't know, Willa," I said. I didn't like the way she was looking at me. Her eyes were too big.

"Come on. Put your pants on. We're going on an adventure."

It was no use arguing with my sister. I'd learned that a long time ago. Ten minutes later, we were staring up at the abandoned movie theater. Willa held Frannie's flashlight, pointing its beam up at the building in front of us.

"This is a terrible idea," I said.

"This is a truly excellent idea."

"It's probably going to collapse on us."

"Louis, if it was really dangerous they'd have torn it down already. It's fine."

Willa couldn't climb the chain link fence that snaked around the building, but she didn't have to. The lock on the gates had rusted and split in two, like someone had taken a shovel to it. Willa danced inside.

"I don't want to be arrested," I said.

"They don't arrest kids with no legs, Louis."

"I have legs."

"That's true. Okay, they'll probably arrest you. But I will bail you out."

"With what money?"

"They don't make kids without legs pay bail money, Louis."

I followed her through the gate.

She walked right up to the front entrance of the building, which was chained off halfheartedly. We obviously weren't the first people to have the genius idea of breaking and entering, because someone had already kicked through the rotting wood of the door. Willa slipped inside easily and then aimed the flashlight back so I could see what I was doing.

The inside lobby of the movie theater was cavernous and dark. There weren't any windows, and Willa's flashlight cast long shadows all over the place. The floor was covered with debris. There were still movie posters on the walls advertising new releases for movies that were now twenty years old.

"Cool," Willa said.

"Can we be done now?"

"Shut up, Louis."

She led us deeper into the theater.

There was no shortage of abandoned buildings in Los Angeles, but the risk of breaking into them did seem, admittedly, higher. This building was in the middle of nowhere. It was creepy, sure, but it seemed relatively safe. In LA, you were breaking into an abandoned building directly next to a Starbucks. You ran a much higher risk of being caught. Still, I was nervous. I could feel my heart starting to speed up, and I tried to convince myself we wouldn't even be here long. Everything was going to be fine.

"Willa, exactly where are you headed?" I asked.

She ignored me, but a few seconds later she turned into one of the theaters. We were on the side of the building that had crumbled away. Half the roof was missing in here, and the screen was sagging on one side. Willa found two seats that were relatively clear of debris, and we sat down. She clicked off the flashlight and when our eyes adjusted, there were the stars.

"I've never seen this many before," she whispered.

"When we went to Joshua Tree," I said.

"This seems different. This is like . . ." She settled back in the seat.

"Like what?"

"You're still having panic attacks?"

I wasn't expecting that. I was expecting something about the stars, something about the sky. I turned to look at her, but it was too dark to see anything other than the outline of her head, the curve of her ponytail. Maybe it was easier that way.

"I don't know what you mean," I said.

"Louis, you're my brother. Why do you keep lying to me?"

"I'm not . . . I'm not lying."

"I know you've been counting. I know you left the diner counting. I know they're happening again, or . . . maybe they never went away?"

"Willa, I don't . . ."

I didn't know how to finish that sentence, so I let it hang in the air until the echo of it had finally faded away.

"We used to tell each other everything."

It was true. We did.

"What else do you know?" I asked.

"I know what a *propensity for self-harm* means," she said.

"You remember that?"

"Yeah. And nobody had to explain it to me. I can feel when you do it. Just like I know you felt it when they cut my legs off."

"It was just like a tickle," I said.

"Only you would call a double amputation a tickle."

She flicked the flashlight on and aimed it at my face.

"Hey!" I said, pushing it away.

"No more secrets," she said. "I mean it. I'm so sick of it."

"No more secrets, fine."

"Promise."

"I promise."

"How can I help you?"

"Geez, Willa, calm down. I'm fine."

"It's worse than I thought. You can't even keep a promise for a minute," she said.

She turned the flashlight off. We stayed in the movie theater for a while longer. If anyone had seen us, they'd have thought we were waiting for the movie to start.

NINETEEN
Frances

When I woke up the next morning, Arrow was doing her meditations on top of the sleeping bag. She'd already showered, and her hair was wrapped in a towel she'd brought from her house. I got out of bed and took a quick, hot shower. When I turned the water off, Arrow stuck a fresh towel into the shower. I wrapped myself in it and stepped out of the tub.

"How are we going to wash these?" I asked.

"First of all, you're welcome from saving you from whatever flesh-eating bacteria is living on these motel towels. Secondly, we'll go to a laundromat, Frannie. Obviously. We're not hooligans."

She left me alone to blow-dry my hair with the dryer she'd brought from home, and by the time I was done, she had already packed up her stuff and was sitting on the corner of the bed, playing on her phone.

"Are you hungry?" I asked her.

"Starving. There's a breakfast place nearby that's supposed to be good."

"I'll hurry."

I got dressed and met Arrow by the car. Arrow had already loaded Kathy up with our things and was behind the wheel waiting for me. The diner was only a few miles down the road, and Arrow drove there quickly, ignoring most street signs for a more do-it-yourself approach to driving. I don't recommend it, but to be fair we were kind of in the middle of nowhere and seemed to be headed only deeper in.

There were a few pickup trucks in the diner's parking lot. Arrow parked Kathy in the shade and we headed inside, our stomachs rumbling audibly the closer they got to food.

The boy behind the counter gave Arrow a particularly interested look when we walked in. He was about our age, and he wore a Rilo Kiley T-shirt that was old and faded and looked suspiciously out of place in the setting.

"You can sit wherever you'd like," he said. To Arrow. I'd turned momentarily invisible.

"Thanks," she said brightly, leading us over to a small booth near the window. The table was wood and covered with a thick laminate that showcased a number of local business cards and flyers.

"What if she changes her phone number?" I asked Arrow, pointing to the business card of a realtor. "Do they order a new table?"

"Probably nobody changes their phone numbers around here," Arrow said.

The boy followed us over and handed us each a menu. "Coffees?"

"Yes please," Arrow said. She hadn't yet noticed that the boy seemed to have forgotten how to blink.

"You have an admirer," I said when he walked away.

"Hmm? Oh, him? He's cute. You know, I think I like Hank Whitney. We seem to have similar priorities."

"Hank Whitney?"

"You stole his handkerchief," she explained.

"You know I didn't steal it," I said. "What kind of priorities?"

"Well, we both like to run. And I've seen him use hand sanitizer, so I'm fairly certain he would never wear a pair of sunglasses he found in a motel room."

I took the glasses off the top of my head now (what? I'd been wearing them) and twirled them around in my hand.

"So . . . about these sunglasses," I said.

"What about the sunglasses you stole? Like you stole Hank Whitney's handkerchief?"

"Actually, I didn't steal them. I had permission to take them."

"Did the previous owner leave a note?"

"No, the previous owner texted me and asked me to bring them back to him."

"You've lost me," Arrow said, turning her attention to the menu.

"Louis. These are Louis's sunglasses."

She looked up at me, poised for some smart comeback, but she was interrupted by our server. He put our coffees down and cleared his throat awkwardly. Arrow looked up at him.

"So my name's Penn, and I'll be taking care of you this morning. Have you had a chance to look over the menu?"

"Are the hash browns like shaved potatoes? Or are they more like a patty?" Arrow asked.

"They're, uh, shaved," he said.

"Perfect. Can I have those with the garden omelet, but can you make sure the hash browns are really well done? Like, burn them. Do not be afraid to make them virtually inedible."

Poor Penn looked virtually about to pass out, but he jotted her order down on his pad. I got a breakfast sandwich and an orange juice.

"So, come again?" Arrow said as soon as Penn had left. "You said these sunglasses are Louis's sunglasses?"

"I did. They are."

"Okay. I'm actually very excited to hear how you think Louis's sunglasses ended up in our motel room in Bluntville, Tennessee. Take it away."

"I can't tell if you're making a joke, but it's Blountville," I said. "And I have no idea. Truly. None. But Louis lost his sunglasses. And I found them."

"And he lost them in . . ."

"California."

"And you found them in Tennessee. Okay. Definitely one possibility. Another possibility: they're not the same sunglasses."

"He said they were the same sunglasses."

"They could be the same brand. Same model, whatever. That doesn't mean they're the same pair. It means it's just a weird coincidence."

Maybe that should have been the first possibility that occurred to me, but it hadn't. I felt slightly let down by the prospect that these weren't actually Louis's sunglasses.

"Oh," I said.

"I don't mean to bum you out," Arrow said. "I'm just trying to keep you honest." She took a sip of her coffee, then squinted at me. "Why do you seem like you care so much? They're sunglasses. You're gross for wearing them, by the way. But they're just sunglasses."

I put them back on the top of my head, using them like a headband to push my hair out of my face.

"You know how . . . I lose things?" I asked, instinctively

lowering my voice. Like anyone in this restaurant might care about my history of misplacing objects.

"Yeah," Arrow said. "I know."

I ignored the skepticism in her voice and said, "It happens to Louis too. The same way it happens to me. Things just disappear for us."

"Okay."

"Disappeared," I said, tapping the sunglasses.

"Reappeared," Arrow said.

"Exactly."

"Your omelet and very burned hash browns," Penn said, placing a plate in front of Arrow. "Your breakfast sandwich and orange juice."

"Thanks," I said, taking the juice. Penn didn't move.

"Can I get you anything else?" he asked.

"No, I think we're good, thanks," I said.

He still didn't move. He watched Arrow take a bite of her hash browns.

"This is perfect," she said. "These are a masterpiece. Compliments to the chef, et cetera."

"I'm glad you like it," he said, breaking into a wide, cartoonish grin.

He still wasn't moving, so I cleared my throat and said, "Is there something we can help you with?"

"Sorry, no," he said, suddenly flustered. "I was just, uh . . . I'm glad you like the hash browns."

Arrow smiled at him. He left in a hurry.

She widened her eyes at me. "So the sunglasses have magically traveled two thousand or whatever miles to end up, magically, on your head."

"You said magically twice. But that is the general theory I'm going with, yes."

"Okay. I mean, like I said, that is one possibility," she said.

"You don't believe me, fine. That's fine."

"I just don't see the point. What would the universe be trying to tell you, you know? You need those sunglasses more than Louis does? Presumably it's pretty sunny in Los Angeles. It's sunny here too."

"I don't know what the universe is trying to tell me," I said. "That's the main problem with my life. I never know what the universe is trying to tell me."

"Allow me to be the voice of the universe this morning." She lowered her voice: "Eat your egg sandwich, Frannie. Drive to Austin. Be kind to your cousin."

"Can we make it to Austin by tonight?"

"Negative. It's still about a seventeen-hour drive. We should have done more yesterday. We're not great at road trips."

"Don't be too hard on us. We're beginners."

When the bill came (Penn placed it in front of Arrow gently, then backed away directly into another table),

Arrow took out her debit card. We were taking turns paying for meals so we didn't have to split everything.

Penn reappeared in an instant and took the check and Arrow's card.

"Maybe he's never seen an Asian person before?" Arrow wondered aloud.

"He just thinks you're pretty," I said.

"He has good taste in music. But he lives in Tennessee, and I do not."

He came back a few minutes later with Arrow's receipt. "So, uh, cool name," he said. "Arrow. Are you, uh . . . I mean, what is your . . ."

"Vietnamese," she said, putting her card into her wallet.

"That's cool. I mean, it's cool you have a Vietnamese name too."

"It's not a Vietnamese name. It's not even a name. It's a weapon. It's not even a Vietnamese weapon. I should have been called Dao." Blank face. "It's like a sword," she said, making a slashing motion through the air. She signed the receipt and handed it back to him. "And your name is Penn. That's not a name either. It's a writing implement. Frannie was stabbed with a pen. Enjoy the rest of your day!"

We left the restaurant quickly. I wondered how long it would take that poor boy to stop thinking about my cousin. Not that I could blame him. Arrow had the natural energy and intrigue I lacked. I'd have a crush on her, too, if she wasn't related to me and I wasn't largely heterosexual.

"I'll take first shift," she offered, heading over to the driver's side.

I was reaching for the door handle when I heard Penn's voice behind us, somewhat frantic and out of breath. I groaned inwardly and turned around.

"Sorry! Ladies! Sorry!" he said, sprinting toward us. He carried a ream of fabric in his arm. Literally. A bolt of blue fabric like you'd get at the craft store.

"Penn?" Arrow asked.

"You ladies forgot your, uh . . . fabric," he said. He looked appropriately confused. He held the bolt of fabric out to me.

"That's not ours," I said.

"It is! I mean, it has to be. It was right in the booth where you were sitting. I went to clean off the table, and it was right there. I'm glad I caught you."

He pushed the fabric into my hands, bowed his head, and jogged back into the diner. I turned the bolt lengthwise and read the sticker on the end of the cardboard.

Linen. HQ. Cerulean blue.

$44.95/yard.

Johar Fabrics.

"Shut the fuck up," I said.

"I didn't say anything!" Arrow said.

"Look at this. Look!"

I handed the fabric over the top of the car. Arrow read the label. "That seems really expensive for linen," she said.

"Johar Fabrics," I said.

"It's not our fabric, Frannie. What do you care where it came from?"

"Louis Johar," I said.

Arrow looked back at the fabric, her forehead knotting in delicate lines. I saw her mouth the words aloud to herself, and then she looked at me and said, "Shut up."

I took the sunglasses off my head and held them. "Do you believe me now?"

Then I slipped them over my eyes and got into the car.

TWENTY
Louis

The first day we'd made it to just outside of Tucson, Arizona, and the second day we took the ten through the city. It felt weird being on the same highway for so many miles and hours. In Tucson, Willa insisted we stop at an auto repair shop. She got out of the car and asked one of the mechanics how much they charged for a shot of Freon. He gave it to us for free.

"CB," I said when she got back into the car.

"And how sweet it is," she replied, turning the air vents toward her face.

We'd gotten a late start. Things were quiet and funny between us. Willa was obviously upset with me for waiting to tell her about the scholarship, even though she'd waited almost a year before telling me about Benson. Willa was funny like that. It probably made perfect sense to her. And I could tell there was something else; she wasn't just mad at me. I thought she was probably upset that Benson hadn't been at the diner, that she hadn't been able to say good-bye to him. She overcompensated for her silence by being, when she did speak, exceedingly polite. She paid for our lunch and apologized for not being able to take a turn behind the wheel.

I'd never been to Tucson before but we left it behind us like we'd left Los Angeles behind us, with the strange resolve that we might never see it again. Willa played with the radio until she found something acceptable, and then she turned the volume so low we could barely hear it anyway.

We'd been in the car for two hours before she turned to me and said, "Isn't this better?"

"Huh?"

"The Freon."

"Oh, sure. Yeah. It's great."

"It's like, one hundred and ten degrees outside."

"No humidity, at least."

"When it's one hundred and ten degrees outside, you're kind of past the point where humidity matters."

We were driving through the desert. Endless stretches of sand and cacti and tumbleweeds. Literal tumbleweeds. Like in the movies.

"There are probably a lot of bodies buried out here," Willa said thoughtfully.

"Come again?"

"You know, like gangsters and stuff. They brought bodies to the middle of nowhere. Who's going to come look for a body out here? It's too hot for digging."

"Gangsters?"

"In the forties and fifties. I mean, we still have them now, we just call them other things."

"You know they finally busted Al Capone for tax evasion."

"I was on the same tour as you," she said.

Alcatraz. San Francisco family trip, three years ago.

"Remember that kid?" I asked.

"Yeah."

He couldn't have been more than six years old. He'd been wearing a bright-red Windbreaker, and he'd walked up to Willa and said, "Those are not real legs."

She'd worn a skirt that fell to her mid-calves and a thick sweater. She had looked around for his parents but hadn't seen them anywhere.

"You are most correct," she'd said. "These are replacement legs."

"How come you have replacement legs?"

"My original legs took a long vacation, but I still wanted to be able to walk and stuff. So I bought these."

"What are they made out of?"

"A bunch of stuff. Like silicone and metal."

"Can I touch them?"

"Sure."

"You won't feel it, though?"

"Nope."

The little boy had put his hands on my sister's fake legs. The kid squeezed his hand around her shin.

"Weird," he said.

"Very weird," she agreed.

"Was it an accident?"

"Michael!" It was the kid's mom. She had burst through a crowd of tourists and grabbed on to Michael's arm, yanking him upright. "I am so, so sorry," she had said to Willa. "Whatever he said . . . He's just a boy. I'm so embarrassed."

"He was just asking questions," Willa had said. "He was very polite."

"They're made out of silicone," Michael had told his mother.

"We'll leave you alone. I'm so sorry. This is mortifying."

"What's mortifying about it?" Willa had said, but the mother had already turned around.

In the car, Willa turned to me and said, "I was going to tell him I was born this way."

"What?"

"If his mother hadn't pulled him away. He asked if it was an accident."

"Why would you lie?"

"You don't want to have to tell kids that shit like this can happen to them. You don't want to make them scared."

"But you don't want to lie to them either. Right? I mean, you've made your thoughts on lying pretty clear."

She laughed. My sister had two laughs. One was a sarcastic, dry bark. The other was nice and light and infrequent. This was the latter, and it shocked me so much that I pulled over to the side of the road and shifted the engine into park.

"What are you doing?" she asked.

"I need to stretch my legs for a minute. I'll keep the air on."

I got out of the car and walked around to the back. We were in the middle of nowhere, and the sun was at the highest point in the sky. It reflected on all the sand and the brightness came from every angle. I started sweating immediately. But it felt good. I didn't like breathing so much chemically altered air. I needed to be outside.

Willa joined me after a few minutes. I watched her struggle to get her feet over the doorframe. I watched her brace herself and pull her body up. I watched her double-check to make sure she wasn't locking us out of the car. She shut her door and walked around to meet me.

"I wish people would realize there's nothing wrong with asking questions," she said thoughtfully, like our conversation hadn't been interrupted. "The problem lies in declaring something is mortifying and then dragging yourself away without further explanation."

"That woman? She was an idiot. She wasn't thinking."

"I disagree. The woman at the diner yesterday—*she* wasn't thinking. Michael wasn't thinking. They were purely instinctual. The host wanted to stare, so she stared. Michael wanted to know what my legs were made of, so he asked. But his mother . . . that requires thinking. She had a conscious thought: *I should be embarrassed. I am embarrassed. I must vocalize my embarrassment.* But the thing that bothers me, you know, is that she wasn't embarrassed by her son. He was just a kid. She must have known he hadn't really done anything wrong. She was embarrassed by *me.* She was embarrassed that I chose to wear clothing that did not cover my prostheses."

Willa paused and gathered her hair up into a ponytail. She was sweating already, beads of water gathering at her temples. She shook her head and said, "Do you know I was spoken to about it? Do you know I had to fight the school for attempting to enforce a separate dress code on me?"

"What? What are you talking about?"

"I was told that it wasn't appropriate for me to wear shorts."

"Everybody wears shorts to school."

"No shit, because it's a hundred degrees every day."

"And they actually told you—"

"'The administration believes it is in your best interest to wear pants or long skirts, so as to avoid providing a possible distraction—'"

"Shut up."

"I'm serious, Louis. We live in this really weird world where female celebrities can be photographed without underwear on and instead of making it illegal to publish explicit photographs of a person without their express permission or, you know, shaming the person who's shoving a camera up their skirt, we call them sluts for accidentally spreading their legs when they get out of their car."

"Willa—"

"And instead of teaching boys to respect girls, we tell girls not to wear tank tops or low-cut shirts. And instead of disciplining the shitheads who called me *stumpy*, we ask handicapped people to cover up their handicap. To pretend they aren't handicapped. To pretend they're whole."

Willa was not crying but her face was red—from the heat or from the anger that was boiling under her skin, I couldn't tell. I put my hand on her hand, and she twitched instinctively underneath my fingers.

"You know why I wear skirts, right?" she asked after a minute.

"Because it's easier for you to walk."

"Yeah. It's easier for me to walk. Pants are too hard to get on. And it's always hot in LA, obviously. And also, there's this part of me . . . Well, I just think it's nice to think that maybe sometime in the past nine years, I passed someone who needed a boost. Like maybe another kid who had an accident or who was born with a handicap or who just felt different for whatever reason, right? And then they pass me and they're like—oh. Look at her. She's not ashamed to show off her fake legs. So I shouldn't be ashamed either. Because there's nothing to be ashamed about. We're all just bodies, right? We're all just fucking bodies trying to move around and work stuff out on our own."

"Jesus, Willa. I just wanted some air."

She took her hand out from under mine and did a slow spin away from me. Then she stopped and looked at me. She raised her arms like she was carrying something. She was smiling, but she also looked like she was Atlas. Borrowing the world for a few minutes so he could have a rest.

"I'm trying to understand," she said.

"Understand what?"

"All that stuff I just said. I really, really believe it."

"Okay."

"But I can't reconcile it with how scared I am to let anyone see me naked."

It was a startling moment of honesty, and I saw my sister blush and turn her head away from me, which made me blush and turn my head away from her, and then a few seconds later we both looked at each other again to see if the other one was looking and we both were, so we laughed.

"Willa," I said. I stepped away from the car. "Go stand in the middle of the road."

"What?" she said, still laughing.

"Trust me. It will look cool."

"It won't look cool," she said, not moving.

"I bet you twenty dollars it will look cool." I took out my phone and opened the camera.

"Okay, but you have to give me twenty dollars."

"I will. I promise."

I directed her over to the middle of the road. She stood in the direct center, on the yellow line. The sun lit her features up in bright orange. My sister got all of the good looks in the womb. She soaked up the beauty and left me awkward and good at tennis.

"Go like this again," I said, and raised my arms. Like Atlas.

She copied me. I took a picture and then brought the phone over to her.

"Damn," she said.

"You owe me twenty bucks."

"That looks really cool."

"I know."

"Uh, fine," she said. She walked back to the car and dug around in her purse and presented me with a twenty-dollar bill. I took it, because a bet is a bet.

"Why are you smiling like that?" she asked.

"Because you're not special," I said. "Because everyone is scared to be naked in front of other people. Not everything has to do with your legs."

The car was still running. It was nice and cool when we got back inside.

TWENTY-ONE
Frances

Arrow made us spend the night in Little Rock, Arkansas. We could have driven farther, but Arrow had a peculiar obsession with Reba McEntire and she put the appropriately titled song on repeat as we drove around looking for somewhere to sleep.

"You know she's not talking about the town, right? She's talking about a wedding ring," I said. "She wants to get a divorce."

"There's a double meaning," Arrow insisted, turning up the stereo.

She sang enthusiastically while directing me down various side streets. She claimed the power of country music would lead us to our destined motel, and she was kind of right because even though it took quite a few detours, we eventually passed the Little Rock, Big Motel.

"This is perfect," Arrow said, gesturing frantically and rolling the windows down. Incidentally she was wearing neon-yellow shorts and a gray T-shirt that said *Let's do this* on the front. She didn't look very country.

"This is where you want to stay?" I asked.

The Little Rock, Big Motel had an enormous, crooked cowboy hat on its roof. The doors were old-fashioned saloon doors. The bike rack had a horse tied to it.

Literally. A horse. Arrow squealed, jumped out of the car, and made a break for it.

"Arrow, don't touch the horse! You don't know where that horse has been!" I yelled, turning off the engine and running after her. The irony didn't escape me that Arrow slept on a sleeping bag and brought her own towels to motels, but she didn't mind running her hands down the side of a strange horse.

"He's so sweet," she said, staring up at the horse.

"How do you know it's a he?" I asked.

"Because he is incredibly well-endowed. What? I didn't go looking for it. It's very prominent."

"Well, thank you," someone said behind us—someone with a lilting, soft voice.

Arrow and I turned around at the same time. The girl was a few years older than us and she wore ripped jeans and a plaid shirt with the sleeves rolled up. Her hair was twisted into a bun on the top of her head. She was smiling without showing teeth. She had two round dimples.

"Is this your horse?" Arrow asked.

"Sure is. This is Vulcan. He's a sweetie." The girl patted the horse firmly on its side. I'd seen people do that in movies but never really understood why. Did horses like that?

"Vulcan? Like *Star Wars*?" Arrow asked.

"*Star Trek*," the girl said, laughing. "But no, actually. He's named after the Roman god of metalworking. His Greek equivalent is—"

"Hephaestus," I finished.

"You really know your mythology," the girl said.

"Hephaestus?" Arrow repeated. "No way."

"My middle name is Hephaestus," I explained. I held my hand out. "Frances. This is Arrow."

"Imelda," she said, shaking our hands one after the other. "Are you on a road trip?" She gestured back to Kathy, stuffed full of enough baggage (and linen, thanks to Arrow) to make it look like we were driving to Oregon.

"We're headed to Austin," I said.

"We're trying to find Wallace Green. Have you heard of him?"

"Of course," Imelda said. "Why are you trying to find Wallace Green?"

"He might be my father," I said, shrugging. "It's kind of a long story."

Imelda's smile faded away for just a second, and then she shook her head and laughed again. "Well, I wish you luck then, Frances Hephaestus. Those movie stars can be tricky to track down."

"Thanks," I said.

"Is this a nice place to stay?" Arrow asked.

"Sure is. My dad owns it. Tell him I sent you and he'll give you a good deal."

Imelda undid Vulcan's ropes and mounted the horse with ease. She smiled at us before the two of them trotted away.

"Imelda is a weird name for a cowgirl," Arrow mused.

"Arrow is a weird name in general," I said.

"Touché. Let's get our stuff!"

We got our suitcases from the car and headed into the motel. The inside looked exactly like walking into a classic Western film, down to the knots of rope decorating the walls and the swinging doors leading to the bar. A little sign above them said *Little Rock, Big Saloon.* The man behind the reception desk was a male, older version of Imelda. He wore a plaid shirt, jeans, and a dirty brown cowboy hat. He wore a name tag in the shape of two cowboy boots. It said his name was Al.

"Hi, there!" he said when he spotted us.

"Hi," I said. "We're looking for a room for the night. Imelda sent us in."

"Good old Imelda!" he said, turning his attention to

a pristine new laptop, the only visible technology in the room. He tapped some words on the keyboard and said, "I'll put you in one of our suites. It has a Jacuzzi!"

"Perfect," Arrow said.

"Dinner is served in the saloon until ten. Will you be needing stables?"

"Oh, we don't have horses," I said. "Just a car."

"No to stables," Al said, tapping on the keyboard again. "Did you see Vulcan, though? Beauty, isn't he?"

"He's really nice," Arrow said. "I've never seen a horse that close before."

"He's a sweetheart. Best horse you could hope to meet. And to think—he was born wild!" he said. "You never know what you're going to get with a wild yearling, but he's been nothing but a gem for the past sixteen years." Al opened a cabinet on the wall; it was filled with tiny gold hooks. Most of the hooks had keys on them. Al removed one and handed it over to me. "Room twelve, darlin'," he said. "Right down that way."

"Thanks," I said. Arrow and I gathered our suitcases and wheeled them down the hallway Al had gestured to. There were doors on either side of us. The room numbers were wrapped in a rope lasso. When we found our room, I slid the key into the knob and twisted it open. We pushed into the room and I flicked the light switch; we were instantly bathed in blinding orange light.

"No *way*," Arrow said, pushing past me. She did two full spins in the center of the room, trying to take everything in. It looked like we'd walked into the set of *Oklahoma!*, the musical. The bed was wood carved to look like a hay bale and the Jacuzzi was placed in the middle of the room. It looked like a wooden barrel.

"What," I said.

"I like this place," Arrow decided, touching a finger to the wallpaper (a field of corn).

"My mother got lost in a cornfield once," I said, rolling my suitcase to the end of the king-size bed.

"Really?"

"With your mom. She never told you about it?"

"I don't think so. But my mom tells really boring stories, so I've gotten pretty good at tuning her out. Sometimes when she's talking, I honestly can't even hear her. Like I can see her lips moving, but . . . silence." Arrow shrugged.

"They were eight or nine," I said. "They were in there for hours."

"Like a corn maze?"

"No, a cornfield. An actual cornfield. Where they grow corn."

"Do you know most of the corn grown in the northeast is actually for cows? It's inedible."

"Humans aren't really supposed to eat corn, anyway. It has no nutritional value."

"Just a place to put butter," Arrow said. "What happened to them?"

"Well, they found their way out. After a while."

"Obviously."

"Grandma had called the police."

"Obviously."

"The end."

"I'll have to ask Mom about it when we get home," Arrow said. She went into the bathroom and shut the door. I heard the fan click on with a deep, alarming rattle.

She hadn't meant anything by it. And I hadn't talked to my mom in years, so it shouldn't bother me so much. But still. I wished I could ask her about it when I got home too. I wished I still had the option of asking my mother about things. I had Arrow and Aunt Florence and Grandma Doris, but I wanted my mom. I didn't have my mom. And I didn't have my dad (either of them). I was alone in Arkansas in a motel room decorated like a cornfield. I felt as lost as my mother felt when she had realized she couldn't see the street anymore.

"That fan is loud," Arrow said, emerging from the bathroom, "but I'm happy to report the bathroom is spotless."

"Does this mean we don't have to sleep in a sleeping bag tonight?"

"Don't be absurd. Let's go get it now and then we can see what the Big Saloon is all about."

I put our room key in my pocket and we headed back to the car. I almost missed the tiny scrap of paper, but the hatchback sometimes stuck so I went around to the driver's side to crawl through from the front and push it open, and there it was. Stuck in the door handle. I unfolded it and read the messy handwriting.

Apart from acting, Wallace Green likes two things: metalworking and horses. He's the guy who sold me my horse years ago. He's a good friend of my dad's. They went to school together. I don't know what it means that I met you tonight, but I don't ignore coincidences. His address in Austin is 3458 Chestnut Hill Drive. I hope you find what you're looking for.

"What's that?" Arrow asked, walking around the side of the car.

"An address," I said.

"Whose address?"

"Wallace Green's address."

Arrow took the note from me and read it to herself, her lips moving slightly. "Huh," she said, handing it back to me when she'd finished. "Isn't that something."

"Isn't that something?"

"Well, isn't it?"

"That girl just handed me Wallace Green's address, and you think it's *something*?"

"I guess he's friends with her dad. Are you gonna help me get this hatchback open or what?"

Arrow walked back to the rear bumper. I put the note into my pocket and opened up the driver's side door. I climbed through the car, putting my knee into one of Grandma's bread loaves. I pushed against the hatchback while Arrow pulled. It came open with a worrying crunch. I half fell onto the gravel driveway and grabbed Arrow by her shoulders.

"What if he's not even my dad? I thought I was doing this for my mom, to prove she was right about him, but if he isn't my dad then isn't this all for nothing? What am I even doing here?"

"You're getting a sleeping bag out of your car," Arrow said calmly, reaching behind me and yanking the sleeping bag out of Kathy.

"You know what I mean," I said.

"Well, nothing is for nothing," Arrow replied, hefting the sleeping bag onto her shoulder.

"That doesn't even mean anything. That doesn't comfort me."

"Well it should," Arrow said. "It's not about the destination, and it's not worth overthinking things. Just accept the address into your life."

"Like you're not overthinking the germs in our motel room?"

"That's different," she said seriously. "Germs can kill you, Frannie."

She air-kissed me. I followed her back into the cornfield and helped her smooth out the sleeping bag on our bed.

TWENTY-TWO
Louis

We drove thirteen hours the second day in the car, and we passed the city limits for Austin just before midnight. Willa had fallen asleep against the window, her mouth open and her legs off and laying in a pile on the floor. They were making her sweaty, she'd said a few hours ago, pulling each one off her and discarding it under the seat. She was asleep almost instantly, snoring softly.

I was tired but I kept driving, propelled by some unexplainable energy that kept my eyes awake and my brain alert. I listened to talk radio and the sound of my sister's deep, heaving breathing. I watched the black road light up in my headlights and then disappear underneath my car, turning momentarily red in my rearview mirror and then returning once more into darkness.

I found a motel outside the city and shook Willa awake after I'd gotten us a room.

"I don't want to put my legs on," she mumbled, her eyes squeezed closed in protest of awakeness. I went around to the trunk and took her wheelchair out, locked it open, and then went to collect her. She held her arms out to me, and I scooped her up easily. She weighed almost nothing. You never realize how much legs weigh until you have to lift someone without them. She put her arms around my neck, and I placed her gently in the chair. "You're a good brother, Louis," she said. I placed her legs on her lap and she cradled them against her stomach.

"You're a good sister."

"No, I'm rotten. I'm a terrible sister. All I do is make you push me around."

"Sometimes you push yourself."

"I liked being in that movie theater. Let's go back there."

"I think you're still asleep."

"What room number are we?"

"Twenty-three."

"That's a strong number. That's a good number. Is it a real key or is it a card?"

"It's a card," I said, dangling it in front of her. She nabbed it.

"Where are our suitcases?"

"I couldn't get you and them. I'll go back to the car in a minute."

"Good guy. Good brother."

I stopped in front of our door, and Willa leaned forward clumsily to unlock it. When Willa got this tired, she seemed drunk, unable to control her body. I leaned forward to catch her left leg, which was sliding off her lap. She pushed open the door, and I rolled her into the room. She found the light switch first and the room was lit up in a yellow orange glow.

"Ohhh," she said, straightening up a little. "A mini bar!"

"Yeah, and everything costs a fortune."

"Oh, please. I'll pay for a little nipper. Don't be so uptight."

She was instantly more awake, taking charge of the wheelchair and bringing herself closer to the fridge. I left her alone and went and got our suitcases from the car. When I got back to the room, she had a tiny bottle of Jameson in one hand. It was half-empty and Willa's nose was scrunched up in distaste.

"Jameson is gross," she said, then took another sip.

"Was there anything else in there?" I asked, pushing the suitcases into the room and locking the deadbolt behind me.

"A bunch of stuff. I just thought I liked Jameson, and I do not like Jameson. But I will finish it. I am not a quitter."

She wheeled herself over to her suitcase and fished

around for pajamas while I knelt in front of the minibar. I didn't want to get drunk, but a tiny bottle *did* seem pretty appealing after a thirteen-hour day of driving. I opened the door of the fridge and reached for another bottle of Jameson (I didn't mind it) when I saw the sheet of thick paper shoved carelessly in the back of the fridge. Assuming it was the price list, I reached over the rows of bottles and slipped it out. It was a thick white paper, torn at the left side like it had been ripped from a sketchbook. It wasn't a price list, it was a drawing of an apple. It was done in charcoal; I ran my finger along the paper and came away with a black smudge on my skin.

"What's that?" Willa asked. She was doing that trick where she somehow got her pajama top over her shirt without showing any skin, and then removed the shirt from under the top. It was kind of like magic. She pulled her bra out through one of her sleeves.

"It's an apple," I said, turning it around to face her.

"Where'd you get that?"

"In there."

"In the fridge? It wasn't in there a minute ago."

"It was behind some stuff, you probably just missed it."

"Uh, no, I moved a bunch of bottles around trying to find some soda to mix with this. Plus I'm pretty fridge-level in this chair. It wasn't in there," she said. "Can you help me on the bed and then close your eyes?"

I put the drawing on one of the two twin beds and then

helped Willa onto the other one. I turned around as she pulled her skirt off and changed into her sleep shorts.

"We should have gotten separate rooms. We're too old to share a room," she said, her voice muffled from lying down.

"We can't afford separate rooms. Plus, we're lucky to find a place that will rent to eighteen-year-olds. I think the law is twenty-one. Plus, we're twins. We lived in the same embryonic sac for nine months. We can share a room."

"That is true. Help me back, please?"

I helped her back into her chair, and she went into the bathroom to wash her face and brush her teeth. I heard her exclaim with pleasure that the bathroom counter was low enough to do both of these things on her own. I picked up the drawing again and studied the apple. It was done with many small, choppy strokes. It reminded me of those dot paintings—George Seurat? Georges? Seurats?—and how much effort they must have taken, how many hours of painstaking brushwork and running back and forth to view it at a distance to check if it's even making sense.

I didn't know much about art, but it was a pretty good apple.

I went to put it on my bed but something stopped my hand. I brought the paper closer to my face and squinted at it. There was a signature in the bottom right-hand corner, tiny and cramped and almost illegible, except I could see a distinct *F*, with arms reaching over a hurried, long *J*.

Willa came out of the bathroom, face red and wet.

"Frances's last name is Jameson," I said.

"So?"

"We're drinking Jameson."

"That's not weird, Louis. It's a popular liquor."

"This is Frances's drawing. This apple. She drew this, and I found it in our minibar."

"You never should have driven so far today. You're clearly hallucinating. You need some sleep."

"Willa, *look*," I said, holding the drawing in front of her face. "Look at the signature."

"Huh," she said. "I mean, that could be anyone."

"Anyone with the initials FJ," I said.

"I guess."

"Look, I didn't tell you. She found my sunglasses."

"I thought you bought new sunglasses. At that weird little gift shop we went to?"

"I did. But Frances *found my old sunglasses*. The ones I lost!"

"No, she didn't."

"Yes, she did."

"That is impossible. Help me into the bed, please?"

I helped her into the bed. She propped herself up on pillows, and I sat down across from her.

"I think something weird is going on," I said.

"Famous last words."

"Willa, I'm being serious."

"I'm being serious too."

"This is Frances's drawing. I know it is."

"If you say so."

"You don't believe me."

"I don't believe that Frances came all the way across the country to leave that drawing in our mini fridge, no, Louis. I do not believe that. I'm sorry if that makes me a bad sister."

"I never said she put it there."

Willa raised her eyebrows. Then she bit the corner of her bottom lip and said, "Okay. What are you saying exactly?"

"I'm saying that this drawing—Frances's drawing—just came to be in our fridge. Like by . . ."

"Are you about to say *magic*?" Willa whispered.

"No, I wasn't about to say magic," I retorted.

I *had* been about to say magic, but then I'd stopped myself because I realized how absurd it would have sounded. And I wasn't even convinced that's what was going on. Something had caused this drawing to appear in the fridge, but I wasn't prepared to give that something a name yet.

"I mean, did you even ask her?" Willa said.

"Ask her what?"

"Like, text her a picture of the drawing and see if it's even hers."

I hadn't, but I got my phone out of my pocket and snapped a picture of the drawing and then texted it to Frances. It was probably too late; she was probably already sleeping. I didn't know where she was in her journey and if there was still a time difference between us. We hadn't texted all day. Should I have been worried that we hadn't texted all day? I sent the picture and wrote:

Is this yours?

Her reply came much later. Willa had already fallen asleep, her arm over her face and her thighs spilling out of the sheets. I had finished the tiny bottle of Jameson, not enough to do anything other than create a welcome, warm feeling in my extremities. I'd turned off the lights and put my phone on the pillow next to my head. I was just starting to fall asleep; I was in that place where the phone's buzzing became a part of my dreams and floated me quietly awake.

The room was lit by the glow of my screen. I picked up the phone and swiped my finger across Frances's name to read her message.

Yes. I don't know what's going on, but yes. That's mine. I never drew that, but it's mine. Pardon the expression, but what the fuck.

I don't know what's going on either. It's a very good drawing.

I can't draw anymore.

Of course you can.

Something is blocking it. I lost something.

Maybe I will find that for you too.

She texted back an emoji. A pink heart with an arrow through it.

I put my phone on silent and went to sleep with it on the bed next to me. The drawing of an apple was on the bedside table.

The first thing I did when I woke up was to check—
And it was still there.

TWENTY-THREE
Frances

We departed Little Rock, Big Motel early the next day and left Arkansas behind us in favor of Texas. It took us about two hours to reach the border, and when we did, Arrow sighed heavily and said, "Ugh, finally, we're almost there. I'm so sick of this car. No offense, Kathy," she said, and petted the dashboard with her free hand. With her other hand, she held a sloppily buttered piece of banana nut bread. She had a line of butter running down the side of her wrist. I had to tell her we were actually, like, four hours away from Austin. (We were, to be perfectly honest, more like six hours away from Austin, but I didn't know how she'd react to that number.)

"What," she said.

"Four hours."

"Nothing in Maryland is four hours away from something else in Maryland. Unless you drive in circles and keep missing your exit."

"Texas is big. Texas is really big."

"Is Texas the biggest state?"

"I think Alaska is the biggest state."

"Is Texas the second-biggest state?"

"I guess, probably."

"Four hours," she said, slumping against the window. "This is torturous."

"Put another podcast on."

"I think if I have to listen to one more episode of *Wait Wait . . . Don't Tell Me!*, I'll turn into a quirky news quiz."

"There are worse things to turn into."

"Ugh, four hours. Okay, fine. I'm committed."

"What would you do if you weren't committed?"

"I don't know. Maybe I'd hitchhike home. I've always wanted to hitchhike."

"People don't hitchhike anymore, do they?"

"Not in Maryland," Arrow said, finishing the last piece of bread. She buttered me a slice without asking and handed it to me. I ate it with my right hand and drove with my left. "What's the first thing you're going to do when you see him?" she asked when I finished.

"I don't know. Probably I'll have to be like—can I have

some of your hair for a paternity test?"

"Oh, I was talking about Louis. But yeah, Wallace Green is important too."

"Arrow, Wallace Green is the main reason for this trip."

"Sure, totally."

"What's that supposed to mean?"

"It means that a trip can have two purposes. This trip specifically can have two purposes. A primary purpose and a secondary purpose."

"The secondary purpose is that I wanted to spend some time with you, okay? Before senior year."

"Bullshit, we spend plenty of time together. We spend too much time together. I'm basically sick of you."

"Fine, whatever. I want to meet Louis. Shut up."

"I will not be silenced," Arrow said. She buttered another piece of bread and broke this one in half. We ate in silence (the irony did not escape me) and then Arrow put on another podcast and we listened to two before deciding to stop for lunch. It was just past noon and hot, but a different sort of heat than I had ever experienced before. This heat was perfectly devoid of humidity. It was a bright, thin heat that didn't get trapped in your hair like the summers of Maryland. It was *nice* to be this hot, even though I started sweating the moment I got out of the car and Arrow walked with bowed legs across the parking lot to "try to get a little breeze up there, Frannie."

We ate quickly and were back on the road within an hour. Even though we got to Austin in good time, pulling into the city limits by five o'clock, I didn't call Louis or Wallace Green. I didn't call anybody except Grandma, to tell her I was still alive and to see whether she was still sitting shiva (she was). And even though Arrow protested and didn't understand why we had even driven this far to sit in a motel room and watch HBO, that is exactly what we did. We sat in a motel room and watched HBO while I felt a rising panic that started deep in my chest and rose up through my throat until it bubbled out through my mouth in the form of a thousand nonsensical syllables.

Arrow looked at me like I might explode. I felt like I might explode.

"Let's go for a run," she said. "I feel like you need to go for a run."

"It's a thousand degrees out."

"We'll take it easy. We'll bring water."

"I didn't pack sneakers."

"Lucky for *you*, we wear the same size, and I brought two pairs."

"Why do you travel with two pairs of sneakers?"

"At this track meet last year, Hank Whitney dropped his only pair of sneakers into a vat of molasses," she said.

"Molasses?"

"We were in Boston, it was a museum, it's a long story. Have you heard about the Great Molasses Flood? Anyway,

I learned my lesson after that."

I did not want to go running. It was maybe the last thing in the world I wanted to do, but I let Arrow throw workout clothes at me and I put them on diligently, stripping off my sweat-soaked driving clothes and leaving them in a heap on the floor.

"I am going to have a heart attack and die," I said, lacing my sneakers.

"You are not. God. You're so lazy. We're basically just going out for a fast walk. Look at it like that."

"Running and walking are totally different things."

"*Running and walking are* . . . Geez, Frannie. Calm down. We're not going to sit here while you hyperventilate all night."

"So we're going to watch me hyperventilate on the streets of Austin?"

"Yes, exactly. You have caught on to my master plan. Now, come. Let us be off."

We were off.

Arrow set a slow, steady pace through the back roads of Austin. I didn't know anything about Austin, but it didn't really look like a city, at least over here in whatever part we were in. I couldn't see any skyscrapers. I was quickly losing my breath and tried to think of a way to distract myself.

"Louis found a drawing I made," I said. "Or, I guess, I didn't really make it. It was a lost drawing. It doesn't make any sense, but he found it."

"Like you found his sunglasses?" Arrow asked, her voice heavy with disbelief.

"I don't know how to explain it, but something is going on."

"Maybe," she said. "Maybe not."

"You have to admit, it's a little spooky."

"I don't have to admit anything." She paused, stretching her hands up in the air. I was out of breath and covered in sweat, but I was determined not to hold her back, so I was keeping my own.

"How come you don't draw anymore?" she asked after another minute or two.

"I guess I just haven't really felt like it."

"You used to feel like doing it a lot."

"Arrow, I don't really know what to say. It's not a conscious thing. I'm just not in the mood."

"When do you think you're going to be in the mood again?"

"You'll be the first to know."

"Well, you don't have to get cranky," she said, turning sideways and running like that for a few minutes.

I had sweat dripping down my face, but Arrow looked dry. She raised her arms up and down in the motion of a bird. Like she was trying to fly away. Then she turned backward and ran looking over her shoulder.

In her form-fitting workout clothes, Arrow was short and lean. Her ponytail was high on her head and bounced in a perky, annoying rhythm. Her feet hardly touched the sidewalk. Mine, on the other hand, slapped against it in a harrowing rhythm until I finally lost my balance altogether and went crashing to my knees.

"Ow," I said.

"Geez, Frannie! Can't you go for one run without mortally wounding yourself?" Arrow said, doubling back and kneeling beside me.

"I'm fine," I said, sitting on my butt. "Oh, look!" I picked a twenty-dollar bill off the pavement and held it up triumphantly.

"Great, you owe me for something," she said, grabbing it out of my hands and sticking it into her pocket. I didn't know how they could get pockets in pants that tight.

I held my hand out to her and she yanked me up.

"Probably we should go back," I said.

"Probably we should walk," she agreed.

I only limped a little. Arrow slung her arm around my shoulders for a bit and then she started jogging circles around me (literally) and then finally she did some cross between a jumping jack and a skip and then eventually, because I was getting dizzy, I put a hand on her arm and stopped her.

"Huh," I said.

"What?"

"It's a pawnshop. I didn't see that on the way out."

"You were too busy panting to death."

"Let's go in. I've never been in a pawnshop," I said.

"Do we have to? It's late and I'm starving."

"Look in the window. It's an original NES, and yours *just* stopped working a week ago. That can't be a coincidence."

I knew I had her. Arrow was a sucker for retro gaming systems. We walked across the street and entered the shop, and she made a beeline for it.

I wandered deeper into the store, passing ancient steamer trunks and a collection of stamps displayed proudly in a glass case. I poked through a small display of sporting equipment, trying on baseball gloves and tossing a football into the air.

I picked up an old tennis racket next. I fished it out carefully and tested its weight in my hand. I didn't know much about tennis rackets, but it looked both old and pristine, in need of new strings but without a scratch on its body. Like it had only been used once or twice.

A small orange sticker on the handle said thirty dollars.

Louis played tennis, and I was sure he already had a racket, but there was something about this one that I liked. It was small and clean and vintage.

"Give me that twenty back," I said to Arrow, who'd come up beside me and stuck her nose over my shoulder.

"Finders keepers," she said.

"I'm the one who found it."

"Oh, fine. You're just lucky that console was incredibly overpriced."

She handed it over. I took the tennis racket to the front and laid it on the counter carefully.

The girl behind the desk glanced up at me with a look of supreme disinterest. Then she looked at the tennis racket.

"Thirty bucks," she said.

"I'll give you twenty," I said.

"Sure, whatever," she said without hesitation. "It's just a tennis racket."

I slapped the bill down on the counter, and she covered it with her hand, sliding it toward her like I might try to grab it back.

Arrow and I left the pawnshop. I held the tennis racket like I had won it. I guess in a way, I had. At least ten dollars of it, anyway. The free ten dollars.

"I've never seen you haggle," Arrow said thoughtfully. "What do you want a tennis racket for, anyway?"

"Louis plays tennis."

"Ohhh," Arrow said. "This is about a boy."

"It's just nice to do things for people, right?" I said. Now that I was out of the store, my confidence of five minutes ago was quickly fading. "Like, people should buy presents for each other, right?"

"Sure, I guess. I mean, does he need a new tennis racket?"

"Technically I think this is an old tennis racket," I said.

"Did he give some indication he might want an old tennis racket?"

"Honestly, not really. I just saw it and thought . . ."

Oh, shit. Why did I buy Louis an old tennis racket? Why did I think Louis might need a tennis racket I'd found in a pawnshop? Why did I do anything I did? What was wrong with me? Was I just going to walk up to him when I met him and say, "Here! I got you this tennis racket! For no good reason I can think of! Because you obviously already have a tennis racket!"

"I guess that twenty dollars was really burning a hole in your pocket," Arrow said. "Even though I was holding it for you. Next time I'll just invest it right away. Get you a savings bond or something."

"Do they still have savings bonds?" I asked, twirling the racket around and around in my hand.

It wasn't the weirdest thing in the world, to give some-one a gift when you met him, right? And anyway, there was something about this racket I couldn't name. It felt good. It had a nice weight. The handle said *Babolat* in gold script. Something nudged at the corner of my brain, like I almost knew something but couldn't quite reach it. But then Arrow took my hand and it was gone, whatever it was.

Arrow made me wash the tennis racket in the bathtub. Shower gel and all. She said I didn't know where it had been, but I thought maybe I actually did.

TWENTY-FOUR
Louis

I woke Willa up early (for her) after a mostly sleepless night (for me). She staggered into the bathroom at ten o'clock, and I called the University of Texas while I waited for her. I'd called them a few days ago and told them to expect me, and they said to let them know when I arrived. *Whenever you get here is perfect*, they'd said. There was someone different on the phone now, but she knew who I was and that made me, for some reason, instantly uneasy. Like they were putting too much importance on me. Was I tricking them into thinking I was someone worth counting on?

And then—should I have brought my tennis racket?

Were they going to ask me to play? Was I going to meet Earl Clarington or Lisa Kent, two of the best young tennis players in the country? Was I going to be forced to play against them? Was this all some elaborate test?

"You're spiraling, aren't you?" Willa said.

I looked up, the phone still held against my ear even though the university had hung up minutes ago. Willa stood in the doorframe of the bathroom. She already had her legs on, and she had a towel wrapped around her. Her hair was wet and uncombed. I hadn't heard her open the door.

"I think this was a mistake," I said.

"You think what was a mistake?"

"Coming here. They don't even know anything about me. I'm probably not at all what they're looking for."

"That is a distinct possibility, Louis. But that's not a reason to bail now. We've come a long way for this."

"I just don't know—like, what if I don't even want to play tennis anymore?"

"Do you not want to play tennis anymore?"

"I don't know. Maybe I never wanted to. Maybe I only liked it because I was good at it."

"For what it's worth, I actually think that's a really good reason to like something," Willa said. "We all want to be good at shit. There's no shame in that."

She went over to her suitcase and pulled clothes out of it until she found something she liked. Then she went into the bathroom again. When she came out, she was toweling her hair dry and I was staring at the phone in my hand.

"You really think that's a good reason to like something? Just because you happen to be naturally talented at it?" I asked her.

"Of course. I could think of a ton of things I would like more if I didn't have to work to be good at them. Practicing sucks. If I could, like, pick up a guitar and be instantly awesome, I guarantee you I would like playing the guitar. As it is, I cannot play a barred chord to save my life, and every time I've tried to change a string, I've poked myself in the face and almost blinded myself."

"Oh yeah, I forgot you had a guitar," I said.

"I sold the guitar," Willa replied, shrugging. "You're lucky, Louis. I mean, I wouldn't necessarily pick tennis to be instantly good at, but at least you have something."

"I wasn't instantly good at it."

"Oh, whatever. You were. Obviously you've gotten better with practice, but you didn't start at zero." She paused a minute, threw her towel on the bathroom floor, and finger-combed her hair. I don't think Willa owned a hairbrush, and I'd definitely never seen her blow-dry her hair before. She gathered it into a low ponytail and then let it go again. "Just don't complain about it, okay? Some of us are zeros at everything."

It was the most disparaging thing I had ever heard Willa say about herself, but she didn't give me time to respond. She aggressively repacked her suitcase, throwing clothes into it without taking the time to refold them. I didn't even tell her that we were staying in the same motel tonight and she didn't need to pack everything. I just watched her go and then followed her outside.

"Willa—" I started.

"Oh, shut up. I'm not, like, devastated I can't play the guitar," she said.

"That's not what I was going to say."

"I get that you're nervous, Louis, I really do. But you have an amazing opportunity here, and the best part about it is that you can do whatever the fuck you want. You can take the scholarship or you can pass it up, and nobody will even be the wiser, you know? You don't ever have to tell Mom and Dad. Your secret will die with me."

"That's really nice of you—"

"But if you're relapsing now because you feel too much pressure to accept this scholarship, you have to let me know. Okay? You have to tell me, or tell somebody. Just know that you can do whatever you want."

I didn't like the word *relapsing*; I didn't like how heavy and deep it felt.

"I'm not . . . I mean, I didn't . . ." I couldn't get the words out. Or, I could get *some* words out, but they weren't the right words. And I didn't know why she was so angry, why it felt like she was lecturing me, but at least it looked like she was calming down. She sighed and pulled open the car door.

"Listen, let's save the heavy shit for later," she said. "We need to go tour a university. Wait—let's get a coffee first and then go tour a university."

She smiled one of those twin smiles, where I knew exactly what she meant—*I'm fine and you're gonna be fine and we're fine. Get in the car.*

I got in the car.

The university representative had given me directions, but I put the address into my phone anyway, and then I ignored everything my phone told me to do in favor of what she had said. This drove Willa crazy, and she spent the car ride drumming her fingers against the doorframe in exasperation, until I stopped and got her a coffee and a muffin, and then she was fine.

I had been told to meet my tour guide in front of the tower in the middle of the campus, which I was worried about finding until we got there and I realized it was a little hard to miss.

"Think you're allowed to go up there?" Willa asked, letting me help her out of the car (she was still tired; she didn't really hit her stride until the early afternoon).

"Probably, sure. I think I read something about an observation deck."

"It's really pretty here," she said. "Not at all what I expected."

"What did you expect?"

"I don't know. A lot of farmhouses."

"You need to get out of Los Angeles more."

"Oh, like you're so world traveled."

Willa and I walked to the tower, passing a series of large white buildings with red roofs and then a fountain with figures on horseback, overshadowed by a woman with enormous, angel-like wings.

"What is that supposed to be?" Willa asked.

"Littlefield Fountain." She shot me a look. "What?"

"For someone who doesn't want to go here, you certainly know a lot about observation decks and fountains," she deadpanned.

"I did some research," I said. "And I never said I didn't want to go here. I said maybe they're wrong about me. Maybe they won't want me."

"I hope that sounds as dumb to you as it does to me," she said.

It did, actually.

There was one more building in front of the tower. We walked around it (with Willa complaining about why we had to park so far away) and saw three small tour groups already gathered together, with parents snapping relentless photographs of the tower as their children pretended not to know them.

"What one are we in?" Willa asked.

I spotted a girl with a clipboard and headed over to her. She brightened when she saw us, and I saw her eyes land only momentarily on Willa's legs.

"Hi!" she said. "You must be Louis. I'm Mary." She held her hand out to each of us and we shook it.

"Sorry, how did you know who I was?" I asked.

"I've seen your picture," she said, like this was normal.

"Gross, you're famous," Willa said out of the corner of her mouth, so Mary wouldn't hear her.

"You can go ahead and join any group you'd like, and then after the tour we're going to bring you around to the tennis courts and have some one-on-one time," Mary said. "Sorry, you're his sister? You look alike."

"Sister, yeah. Willa. Nice to meet you."

"Great! Here, um, here's my number. Sometimes the groups get back at different times, so call me whenever the tour is done, and I'll meet you back out here." Mary scribbled her number on a piece of paper on her clipboard and then ripped a piece off and handed it to me.

"Thanks," I said.

"Sure thing! See you later."

Willa and I joined the smallest group and I took my phone out of my pocket while I waited for the tour to begin. I'd missed a text from Frances a few minutes ago.

Austin is hot.

I'm here, too! Starting a tour at the university.

I guess I'm going to try calling Wallace Green in a minute. That's weird.

Pretty weird. Keep me updated. Dinner tonight?

Yeah. I'll text you later.

I put my phone away and said, "I guess we're having dinner with Frances tonight."

"Are *we* having dinner with Frances tonight, or are you having a little date with Frances tonight?" Willa retorted.

"I don't know. Shut up."

"Did she meet Wallace Green yet? Did she weasel her way into his inheritance?"

"That's not why she wants to meet him."

"I know, Louis, *relax*. I was kidding. Obviously she wants to meet him because she has dreams of being a famous movie star and she thinks he can get her in the biz."

"You're impossible."

"I was still kidding. But did she meet him? How do you even find a movie star? Is she just walking up and down the streets of Austin yelling his name? Do you think that would work for me and Michael Pitt?"

"I think Michael Pitt lives in Brooklyn."

"I know, I'm thinking ahead. Next road trip! What if

we didn't go back to high school, what if we just kept going on road trips?"

"We would run out of money."

"Well, obviously we would sell our internal organs for funds. Gosh, you're so uninventive. I need a better road-trip partner."

"Do you want another coffee before we start? I could go get you another coffee," I offered.

"Are you trying to get away from me?" Willa asked suspiciously.

"You're just talking a lot. I think it might be nice to have some quiet time."

"I don't even have to go on this tour. Do you not want me to go on this tour? I don't even care," she said.

"Okay, I think that's about everything! Let's get started!" the tour guide said, cupping his hands around his mouth for projection.

I grabbed Willa's hand. "Of course I want you to come on this tour, Willa. I'm fucking terrified."

Willa smiled smugly. She removed her hand from mine but squeezed me gently around the side. "Talking incessantly kind of gets your mind off it, though, wouldn't you say?"

Whenever I think I have figured my sister out, she goes and does something I didn't see coming.

Then she handed me her empty coffee cup. That, I could have predicted.

I jogged over to the nearest trash can and threw it away. When I turned around, I saw a small square of white fabric on the ground. I bent over to pick it up. It was a handkerchief with the initials HW embroidered in blue thread in one corner. It was near where Mary had been standing with her clipboard. A boyfriend's? An ironic vintage accessory?

But then I remembered something Frannie had written in one of her messages, something about losing a handkerchief from a boy named Hank Whitney.

HW.

I mean . . .

It couldn't have been a coincidence, right?

I put the handkerchief in my pocket and rejoined Willa with the tour.

"You're missing it," Willa said. "The tour guide is extolling the virtues of the tower. It is three hundred and seven feet tall."

"Fascinating," I said. I meant it to come out like I didn't care, but I failed miserably. Willa smiled and nudged me with her shoulder.

"It's pretty cool," she agreed.

The rest of the tour was equally pretty cool.

TWENTY-FIVE
Frances

I was awake.

It was early—seven in the morning—and I had been up for two hours already. Arrow slept in the sleeping bag next to me, and I stared up at the ceiling, getting intimately acquainted with the fire sprinkler directly above our heads.

After our failed run last night, Arrow and I had come back to our motel room and watched more HBO, and I tried not to freak out about the fact that Louis and I were both in Austin at the same time and I had found his sunglasses and he had found a drawing of an apple that I had never done. That I was unable to do.

And what was I even doing here? What was I supposed to do now?

Was I calling Wallace Green, was I showing up at his address? I'd plugged the address Imelda gave me into Google. There were aerial pictures of his property and even a video tour from a time he'd done one of those in-depth interview specials from his living room. I now knew the walls of his kitchen were painted a bright, cheerful blue and his favorite room in his house was one painted bright red, every inch of wall space covered with shiny, priceless acoustic guitars.

"I don't play much music," he'd told the interviewer, and then he'd grinned for the camera. He'd had a cowboy hat pulled low on his forehead (I wanted to hate that cowboy hat, I really did, but I couldn't deny the appeal). "But I have a lot of talented friends. And I like how these guitars look. Don't these guitars look nice?"

It should have been easy to hate Wallace Green, but he was so damn happy all the time. And he'd given away so much money that he'd officially been taken off the Forbes list of richest people. And he'd chosen to live away from Hollywood and in the city of his birth. And his house was huge but it wasn't exorbitant, if you considered what he could have afforded instead. And he was just so *happy*. And there was no controversy in his past either. You searched his name on the internet and the only thing that came up was pages and pages of how Wallace Green is basically the best human being to ever grace the surface of the earth.

And maybe he was my father.

No pressure.

I nudged Arrow awake. I couldn't stare at the ceiling anymore. I itched to get out of the motel room, to go explore, to do anything except listen to the sound of our breathing.

"Lee-me alone," Arrow mumbled, turning over and pressing her face into the pillow.

"Wake up, Arrow," I insisted, digging my elbow into her side. "I need to talk to you."

"Frannie, I'm dead. I'm tired. I'm dying," she said, lifting her face from the pillow so I could hear what she was saying. "Unless you are similarly dying and need my immediate assistance, please leave me alone. Because my alarm is set for eight and it hasn't gone off yet, so I know it's earlier than eight and that's just stupid. And . . . Oh, shit, now I'm talking too much. I'm awake. Shit, Frannie, you're so annoying." Arrow rolled onto her back and stretched her arms out in front of her. "What do you want? This better be good. If it isn't good, make something up."

"I need to know what you think is going on."

"What's going on with what?"

"I couldn't sleep. I just kept thinking about what the hell we're doing here, and what the hell Louis is doing here, and what the hell does this even mean?"

I pulled up the photograph of the apple drawing on my

phone and showed it to her. She squinted at it, her eyes still fuzzy from sleep, and then she shrugged.

"Is that—"

"It's the drawing Louis found. My drawing."

Arrow sat up in bed. I sat up in bed. We sat across from each other, legs folded, staring.

"You asked me why I don't draw anymore. I don't know. I was in art class four months ago. The teacher told us to draw an apple. I didn't. Or else—I couldn't. I don't know which. And then I just couldn't draw anything. I tried, but I couldn't make my hands work. I couldn't even doodle. I failed art."

"You *what?*" Arrow said.

"I failed art," I said. It was the first time I had said those words aloud, the first time I had really let myself think about it. I had failed art. The only class I even cared about. The only thing I had that I liked, that I was good at. I had always had my art, through the stabbing and through the divorce and the legal proceedings, through losing my mom and going to live with my grandparents. I had always had art and then I didn't have it anymore, because I couldn't draw an apple, and because I couldn't recover from not being able to draw an apple.

"Grandma and Grandpa know you failed art?" Arrow asked.

"No."

"But they had to sign your report card. That's policy.

Guardians have to sign off on failed classes."

"Do you know when the school finally got around to sending those forms out?" I said. Arrow shook her head slowly, but then changed her mind and nodded.

"You braved a bite from a black widow spider to get that form before they did," she guessed. "And you found the letter from the Easton Valley Center."

"Imagine my surprise," I whispered.

"I'm so sorry, Frannie."

She reached across the bed and grabbed my knee. I remembered that day, just last week, when I had opened the mailbox. Part of me had expected the spider to be there, waiting. But there had never been a spider. Of course there had never been a spider.

"What are you sorry about?" I asked her. "That they lied to me, or that I found out the way I did?"

"I guess . . . both. I'm sorry for both. I'm just sorry."

"It's fine. I just want some breakfast. I want some pancakes."

"I have to meditate."

"Meditate quickly, okay? I'm going to jump in the shower."

I showered while Arrow meditated, and then she showered while I got dressed, and then I waited while she got dressed, and then we got in the car and drove until we found a diner.

"Look okay to you?" she asked, pulling in front of a

small, sky-blue building with white shutters. It was entirely out of place in the neighborhood. A shabby-chic sign called it Debbie's Diner.

"I'm starving. Looks great," I said.

Arrow turned the car off and fed the meter, and we walked around the side of the tiny building. The door was propped open with an old dress shop mannequin.

The inside of Debbie's Diner was decked out like a sewing room. There were antique sewing machines bolted to the walls and a collection of pincushions overcrowding a tall, glass-fronted armoire. Large, embroidered tapestries covered the far walls: elaborate scenes of kittens playing with balls of yarn and puppies napping in wicker baskets.

"Holy crap," Arrow said, and I knew she meant it in the best way possible. Her eyes were wide and her mouth was open. Arrow loved kitsch; she was in her element.

"This is something, huh?" I said, trying to humor her.

"Give me my camera," she hissed.

Arrow didn't have a camera, so I knew she had fully committed to an alternate version of reality. I gave her a high five instead of a camera (she was holding her hand over her shoulder), and we took a seat in one of the open booths, as per the *Please Seat Yourself* sign.

There were two menus already on the table, so I took one as a server came over (Debbie herself? One could only hope) and set coffee down in front of us without asking if we wanted it.

"You ladies just holler when you see something you'd like, all right?" she purred (she sounded like a cat, she looked like a cat, and she was wearing a knitted sweater with cats on it), setting a tiny pitcher of cream between us.

I looked up at Arrow, who appeared suddenly crestfallen. "What?" I asked.

"I thought she'd say 'y'all.' I thought everybody here would say 'y'all,' and so far nobody has," Arrow said. She turned her attention to the menu, shaking her head slightly in what I knew was the sincerest of disappointments.

I opened my own menu, and a loose piece of paper almost fell out. It looked like a permission slip of some kind, or else a doctor's office form, one of those emergency contact sheets you have to fill out every time you go to the doctor, even if nothing has changed. I scanned the filled-out information and actually felt my heart skip a beat when I saw his name.

Louis Johar.

That's the weird thing about hearts.

They speed up or slow down. They skip beats. They don't behave. They get in the way.

I put my menu down and read the paper more carefully. It was an emergency contact form. It was filled out in Willa's handwriting (I just knew this, which remarkably didn't even register as weird) and listed her brother as her emergency contact. At the bottom, in defiant, messy script, she'd written *Go green*. With the period.

"What, are those the specials?" Arrow asked, reaching for the paper. "I didn't get them; let me see."

"It's not a specials list," I said, letting her take it.

She read it more than once. I saw her eyes scanning across the page. She handed it back after a minute.

"Why would you bring that to a restaurant?" she said. "Where did you even get this?"

But she said it in such a way that I knew she knew I hadn't brought it to the restaurant. I knew she knew I had found it in between the covers of my restaurant menu just like I had found a twenty-dollar bill and used it to buy a tennis racket in a pawnshop.

I didn't know. And I didn't know where to put any of this stuff. Not physically put it, obviously, I put it in my car. I packed it up in my suitcases. But mentally—where did I put it mentally?

For years and years and years I had lost everything. Stacks of letters and packs of bubble gum and a Super Soaker I had begged my mom to get for *months* ("We are not a family that supports *guns*, Heph, not even ones that shoot water instead of bullets, okay?") and then lost immediately, practically midsoak; one second I was drenching Arrow in streams of beautiful, concentrated water and the next minute I was empty-handed and wailing and miserable, knowing I would never convince my mother to buy me a replacement, not when the original had been so hard to come by.

But now instead of losing things I was gaining them, but they weren't even my things to gain, they were all Louis's. They belonged to someone else, someone I had never even met, unless you could count hours of late-night instant messaging or doctor-prescribed group counseling sessions—and I wasn't even sure you *could*. I mean, was I crazy for thinking it might be a good idea to meet him in person? Was I setting myself up to be ax-murdered? Was I setting myself up to be, at the very least, vastly disappointed?

"Are you okay?" Arrow asked. "They have fourteen different kinds of pancakes."

"I think I'm losing my mind," I said. "Just like them."

"No," she said seriously. "It skips a generation. Don't have kids. You're okay."

"I haven't lost anything for *days*," I said.

"That's a good thing!"

"No, I mean . . . That's it. I haven't lost anything for days. That means I'm going to lose something big. My brain. My mind. I'm losing my mind. That's how this ends," I said.

"That's how what ends?" Arrow asked. She tried reaching across the table, but I pulled my hand back. I folded the emergency contact form and put it into my pocket.

"I don't know," I said. "Forget I said anything. I want banana and chocolate chip."

"Frannie—"

"I'm fine."

"You don't seem fine. You don't really think that's a possibility, do you?"

"It has to be," I whispered. "Of course it is. I mean, that's the whole reason Grandma and Grandpa didn't tell me she was at Easton Valley."

"Well, they were wrong, obviously. We've already established that. They should never have kept something so huge from you."

"Maybe they have a point. Maybe I wouldn't have waited until now to realize this was a possibility, you know? Maybe I would have spent the past five years—"

"Having a relationship with your mom? Going to visit her? Frannie, in no universe do they have a point," Arrow said sharply. "And if you're worried about this . . . Well, I think it wouldn't be a bad idea to talk to someone about it. Someone else, I mean, who knows something about this kind of thing. Like a therapist. A psychologist."

I heard Arrow talking as if she were in a tunnel, far away, as my mind raced through all the terrible possibilities I had never really considered before. Was schizophrenia genetic? What had caused my father to snap? Was I helpless, doomed to turn out the same way they had?

"I guess so," I said, only because I knew Arrow was waiting for an answer from me. My heart was beating out of my chest. I thought of those cartoons where anthropomorphized animals fell in love and their hearts popped out of their bodies, *boom, boom, boom.*

"And, Frannie, your mom needed help for years before she was admitted to Easton Valley. Your father was obviously the same. You're not them. Recognizing the need for help is already so much of the battle. You're going to be okay, no matter what happens." Arrow reached across the table and squeezed my arm. "Also, we're in a restaurant filled with embroidered cats. We need to make the most of it."

She flagged down the server and ordered pancakes for us both as my heart slowly calmed down and returned to its proper position inside my chest.

TWENTY-SIX
Louis

After the public tour of the grounds and private tour of the tennis courts, Willa and I headed back to the tower and went up to the observation deck. We leaned over the balcony and Willa took a hundred panoramic iPhone photos of the view. It really was a beautiful campus.

I walked the length of the balcony and then turned to walk along the next side when I saw it, a stack of letters wrapped in brown twine, placed carefully on the floor in a corner no one was paying much attention to.

I looked around but nobody was watching—it was only Willa and me up there, which was maybe strange or maybe not. I gathered the letters carefully, reading the return address even though I already knew what it would say: Easton Valley Rest and Recuperation Center for the Permanently Unwell.

And then I looked at the addressee. Instead of "Frances" it said "Heph," but I knew what that meant because I knew her middle name. And I knew her mother always called her Heph. And I found myself feeling incredibly sorry for her because she had lost these letters and even though I was supposed to meet her in an hour, I didn't feel right holding them. I didn't want to have them for a minute more than I was supposed to.

I couldn't even enjoy the view.

The letters burned into my hands.

They were hot, and I tried to tell myself that was only because they were sitting directly in a shaft of early evening sun and they had probably been sitting there for hours with nothing to do other than soak up the warmth of the Austin day.

But it was a different kind of heat. Or at least it felt different to me. I held the letters in my hand and then put them into the University of Texas tote bag Mary had given me after she'd shown me the tennis courts. They settled against a University of Texas T-shirt and a University of Texas pen and a University of Texas brochure.

"Damn," Willa had said when she'd peeked inside. "Really pushing the old Longhorns on you, eh? Eh? And the color orange? Orange doesn't look good on us, anyway.

You're screwed. Screwed and tattooed. Ohh, we should get tattoos!"

I kept the tote bag pressed against the side of my rib cage, letting the warmth from the letters burn through the canvas and into my skin. I was worried it might catch on fire.

"What are you doing, nerd? You're missing the sunset," Willa said.

"The sun is nowhere near setting," I answered.

"Right, whatever, but the sky is beautiful and you're missing it. Why are you missing it?"

"I was just thinking. We have to leave soon anyway. We're meeting Frances and Arrow for lunch."

"You mean for dinner?"

"For dinner."

"Ohhh, you're nervous. Only nervous people say lunch instead of dinner."

"I'm not nervous, I'm just contemplative."

"Oh, you're *contemplative*. My bad."

"It's like you try to make things harder for me."

"Not harder. Just more honest. I think everyone should be more honest."

"Oh, is that why you broke up with Benson instead of telling him you weren't ready to have sex? Because you're so committed to an honest lifestyle?"

I knew it was the wrong thing to say even before I said it, and I could have stopped but I didn't; I forged onward just to see the look on her face, because honestly I was just a little sick of her self-righteousness and her needling me about Frances over and over again. Willa preached a lot, but she was just as confused as I was, especially when it came to relationships—even though I knew I couldn't call what Frances and I had a relationship, at least not in the same way as Willa and Benson.

Willa smiled.

It was a confusing smile. It wasn't happy, obviously, but it also wasn't overly dangerous. She put her elbow on the railing and leaned against it.

"Touché, brother," she said.

"What, that's it?"

"I mean, I can't really argue with you, if that's what you were expecting."

"Not expecting. Just. I don't know. I'm sorry I said that."

"Well I'm not sorry I made fun of you for saying *contemplative*. And I'm not sorry you said that either. It's the truth. I'm telling you to be honest with no intention of being honest myself. That makes me a hypocrite, and hypocrites suck."

"You don't suck, Willa."

"Oh, I know. Just that small part of me," she said. "Come on, let's go. We have a dinner to make."

I knew Willa was tired after a day spent walking from one end of the campus to another. She walked slower than usual back to the car, and she even looped her arm through mine for support. My phone buzzed in my pocket, and I knew it was probably Frances texting to see if we were still on, but I didn't check it until Willa was in the passenger seat. Then I reached into my pocket, but Willa put her hand on my wrist before I could pull my phone out.

"Would you hate me if I didn't want to go?" she asked.

"To dinner?"

"I'm just so tired. This campus is enormous. My legs are chafing," she said. She fanned herself with a map of the United States that my mother had insisted we bring but that we hadn't once used, because paper maps didn't have voice guidance. "And I don't want to roll up in a wheel-chair, you know? Literally roll up, by the way, that was very funny and I didn't even try. I don't know, would you hate me? I'll go if you really want me to go. I don't want you to hate me."

At that point, I guessed what Frances's text said but just to confirm, I pulled my phone out of my pocket and read it.

> Arrow wants to bail. Guess I'm meeting just
> you and your sister alone?

I felt pressure like it was a real thing with actual weight, a thing that settled itself on my shoulders and made my neck hurt. I hadn't wanted this to be a date. I'd wanted this to be easy, uncomplicated. But now Willa was tired and Arrow, for whatever reason, had decided not to go and I couldn't cancel on Frances. I couldn't come all the way to Austin and not see her, not even find out if she'd met Wallace Green and if he was her real father or not. That was the shittiest thing I could imagine. I texted her back:

> **Willa doesn't want to go either. I'll see you in 30.**

"The suspense is killing me," Willa said. "Are you texting an executioner? Is that how much you hate me?"

"It's tempting, but no. I'll drive you back to the motel."

"Oh," she said, her face falling suddenly, clearly remembering that she'd packed up the entire motel room in a fit of semi-rage this morning. "Oh, shit. Well at least it was a dramatic exit. Ugh, I was super cranky this morning. I'm sorry, Louis. But yes, drive me back. Please and thanks."

So I drove Willa back to the motel and helped her unpack again ("Not like I'll actually need any of my stuff because I intend to watch TV for five hours straight before falling asleep in my clothes.") and then I set off to meet Frances at a place called Holdem.

Like Texas Hold'em, I guessed, although I hated poker and thought it was probably spelled Hold 'Em, anyway. Or Hold-em. Or—

I was panicking.

I could feel my heart beating much too quickly in my chest. I gripped the steering wheel until my knuckles turned white (that was always happening in books, and it was happening now, I had never seen the bone so clearly through my skin before). I tried to remember the last time I had been this nervous. I'd taken Tara Flower to the junior prom, and that had been nerve-wracking but not insurmountable. This, though. This felt insurmountable.

Even as I pulled into the parking lot of the restaurant and parked and shut off the engine and got out of my car and put one foot in front of the other until the door was right there, right within my reach, it still felt like an impossible journey. I paused with one hand outstretched, unable to find the doorknob. I could *see* it, I just couldn't make my fingers cross that last tiny hurdle, those last few inches of air. I watched my hand not moving and then I let it fall to my side and then I heard, in a voice that was at once soft and also a hundred times braver than I currently felt, "You're not gonna pass out or anything, are you?"

And I turned and it was her. Of course it was her. She wore jean shorts that were frayed and sunbleached and a baggy T-shirt and her hair was pulled into a ponytail. She was smiling a little hesitantly, like she was afraid I wouldn't smile back. Like she was afraid of me, or of something I might do.

"Because it's pretty hot," she said after a minute. "I had to listen to Arrow's hydration speech three times today.

Oh—she's not coming. She said she needed to go for an actual run, without me slowing her down."

I found my voice if only because I was acutely aware of how murdery I would appear if I didn't speak. "Oh. Hi." It wasn't Shakespeare, but I thought it was a fairly appropriate response.

"Hi. It's nice to meet you." And then she stuck her hand out a little too far and jabbed me in the stomach. And then she laughed and shook her head, like she could maybe physically shake awake her nerves—or maybe that was just wishful thinking on my part, so I shook my head too—and then I shook her hand. It felt exactly like I would have guessed her hand would feel. But I can't really explain it.

"It's nice to meet you, Frances."

"Oh," she said. "Call me Frannie. Do people call you Lou? These are the weird sorts of things that never come up if you only talk to someone under the moniker of a screen name." Her smile was unfair. Like, too big to comprehend.

"Louis," I said. "I had an uncle named Lou, and he smelled like a fish tank."

"For any particular reason?"

"Well, he owned a pet store. I also just didn't like him."

"So Louis."

"Louis, yeah."

"Well, are you hungry?"

"I'm starving. Are you hungry?"

"Yes. I picked this place because it's not a steakhouse. There are a lot of steakhouses around here."

"It looks great."

Frances turned to go inside, but I put my hand on her arm. "Oh, wait a second. I have this." I was still carrying around the University of Texas tote bag. It was bright orange and featured the Longhorns logo on one side. I was carrying it so the logo was against my rib cage.

I reached into the tote and pulled out the apple drawing. She took it from me like it was a potentially dangerous thing. Like it might bite her. She held it in front of her and looked at it, and I had more things in the tote to give her but I waited.

"Charcoal," she said after a minute.

"What?"

"I never draw with pens. It's all smudgy now."

She touched the drawing and when she pulled her hand away, her fingers were dusted with black.

"I'm sorry," I said. "I should have put it in something. Like a bag, or . . ."

"Oh, no, that's not what I meant. I just meant . . . I guess I should get over it. I guess I should draw with pens sometimes. They're more permanent." She held the drawing down at her side like she couldn't look at it anymore but didn't want to let it go. "But I haven't really drawn anything for a while. So maybe it doesn't matter anyway."

I dug around in the tote bag for the University of Texas

pen I'd gotten after the tour. I held it out to her and said, "I don't have anything to draw on."

She smiled and took the pen, looking at it for a minute like she was trying to decide if it was okay, if she was okay with it. Then she turned the apple drawing over and laid it on the ground, clean side up. She knelt down in front of the restaurant door, and I bent down beside her.

"What should I draw?" she said.

"An apple," I said, because it was the first thing that popped into my head, because the original drawing had smeared so badly.

And on the ground in front of the restaurant she started to draw, her hand moving so fast but so deliberately, a small blur as it curved around and around the page. I watched the still life emerge from nothing, from blank space to perfect apple in front of my eyes. It was just a quick sketch but it felt important, it felt like so much more.

When she was done, she held it up with a flourish and then laughed and signed her name and gave it back to me.

"Keep it," she said. "It's my gift to you."

"I have more for you," I said, pulling the handkerchief out of the bag and handing it to her.

"HW," she read.

"Is that the one?"

"This is the one." She paused, smiling, looking at it, then remembered: "I have some things for you too. They're in the car."

"Just one more," I said before she could go and get them. I withdrew the stack of letters from the tote bag. I handed them to her, but it was a minute before she took them. She stared at them in my hand like she was trying to figure out what they were. But of course she knew. She had to know.

"You didn't—" she started.

"Of course not," I said. "I would never."

"I shouldn't have even asked."

"It's okay. You can ask me anything."

I hadn't meant to say that.

Frances took the stack of letters from me. Her hands were shaking. She thumbed through them quickly; I could see her mouth moving as she counted them.

"They're all here," she said, her shoulders rising as she brought them to her stomach in something a little bit like a hug. She let out a sigh of relief. "Shit. I thought they were gone forever. And they're the only thing I really have of her." She paused like she might elaborate, but then she just held the letters up and said, "Thank you. For these. I really appreciate it. And I'm not hungry anymore. Are you hungry? I don't know. Maybe we can go for a walk?"

"Actually, a walk sounds great. I'm not that hungry either."

"Let me just put these in my car," she said.

I followed her to her station wagon. She put the letters and the apple drawing on the passenger seat and then she rummaged around in the back for a minute before withdrawing a pair of sunglasses, a bolt of fabric, a piece of paper, and . . . a Babolat tennis racket.

My Babolat tennis racket.

I ignored everything else and reached for the racket first.

It was warm.

My hand brushed against Frannie's hand.

That was warm too.

Everything was warm.

TWENTY-SEVEN
Frances

Arrow and I had been sitting in front of Wallace Green's house for twenty minutes, and for twenty minutes Arrow had been trying to get me to tell her about my night with Louis. I was enjoying coming up with more and more complicated reasons of why I didn't want to tell her, mostly because it kept my mind off the fact that we'd been sitting in front of Wallace Green's house for twenty minutes and I wasn't yet ready to address that.

"I think there are things that should exist only in your memory, or only in the shared memories of two people. And if one of those people breaks the unspoken code of silence and shares those memories with another person, it is only doing a disservice to what should never have been spoken about again. So in conclusion, that is why I refuse to tell you about last night."

Arrow looked venomous.

It was a feat for Arrow to look venomous, because her face was usually so soft and so happy. The muscles weren't used to forming the extreme scowl they found themselves in now. As a result, her face looked more funny than anything. But I didn't laugh. I knew better.

"Frances," she said, "are you fucking kidding me?"

"I told you all the important things. We met for dinner. He gave me the letters. We decided to skip food and go for a walk instead. It was really nice. I had a really nice time. Nothing happened."

"I love you so much. I would do anything for you. You're my oldest friend and my legal relative. But at this moment, I just want you to be perfectly clear on this, I could kill you. Okay? I am a nonviolent person, but I am admitting that somewhere deep inside me, the nonviolence is losing to the extreme desire to hit you over the head with my muffin."

"Well, you'd have to do more than that if you want to do any real damage. I think my head's tougher than a muffin."

"It's a really stale muffin," Arrow said, her disappointment momentarily shifting from my unwillingness to share the details of last night to her muffin, which was beyond really stale and moving toward inedible.

The truth was, I didn't feel like talking about it for exactly the reason I'd said. Because it was one of those nights that felt so perfect and so contained within itself, and talking about it with someone who wasn't there ran the risk of cheapening it or tainting it with an outside perspective. I didn't want an outside perspective. I wanted to keep it as close to me as I could. I wanted to keep it so close to me that it was inside me. Just me and Louis and the streets of Austin and the heat of the night and the way he did not put the tennis racket in his car, just held it as we walked and swung it around in his hand and looked at it like it was much more than an impulse decision I'd purchased at a pawnshop.

Here are the things that I will say about it: it was sweet, it was quiet, it was perfect. I wished I was back there now, because I felt safe in every respect, and I did not feel safe now, sitting in the hatchback of my station wagon parked across the street from Wallace Green's house, which was I guess technically a mansion, although I couldn't see it from the road. There was a fence that looped around the entire property and at the gate was a call box.

Arrow ate her stale muffin next to me and drank a coffee. She hadn't gotten me anything because I hadn't wanted anything and because she was mad at me. I understood why she was mad at me, but if I had to tell the truth, I also didn't care.

"How long are we going to sit here?" she asked. "Just so

I can prepare, you know."

"You could have gotten me a muffin," I said.

"You said you didn't want a muffin."

"You could have gotten me one anyway. You usually get me one anyway."

"Next time I run into a coffee shop and you say you don't want anything, I'll be sure to use my mind-reading powers to see if you really don't want anything or you're just being difficult."

"Great, thanks. And we're going to sit here until I stop feeling like I'm going to puke. Okay?"

"Okay, fine. See if I care."

I jumped off the back of the station wagon and went around to the driver's side. I'd left my phone on my seat; I reached through the rolled-down window to grab it, and that's when I noticed the cup of coffee in the cup holder. I opened the door and grabbed it. Still warm too.

"Hey, you're not all bad," I said, joining Arrow with my coffee and my cell phone. "Thanks for the coffee."

"I said I didn't get you anything," Arrow replied.

"Actually, I have something for you too." I'd put Hank Whitney's lost handkerchief in my pocket that morning. I took it out now and gave it to her. She regarded it suspiciously.

"HW," she said, reading the embroidery.

"Indeed."

"Where did you get this?"

"Louis found it on the university campus."

"No, he didn't."

"He did. One day you'll stop doubting everything I say."

"That remains to be seen," she said. I watched as she folded the handkerchief slowly, slipping it into her pocket like it was a lot more delicate than it was.

I took a sip of the coffee, burned my tongue, and wanted to die. Not because I'd burned my tongue. Because I was suddenly so nervous that my insides felt like they were going to hemorrhage and melt and leak out through a hole I'd cut in my shin while shaving my legs that morning.

"What am I supposed to do now?" I whispered.

"You're supposed to go up to that call box and press some buttons," Arrow said. "Because we're here. We drove all the way to Austin and some cowgirl gave you his address and here we are and now you have to do something about it. It's time to step up, Frannie. I got your back." She took a bite of her muffin and then looked sideways at me. She rolled her eyes and hugged me without warning. And hard.

"Ow," I said.

"I can't be mad at you. I think you're a jerk, but whatever. Let's do this."

We slid off the back of the car, and Arrow closed the hatchback. She threw her empty muffin bag on the driver's seat, and we crossed the street together. I was shaking. I was practicing what I would say.

Hello, Wallace Green. I'm Frances. Do you like metalwork-ing? I think I might be your daughter.

"Take a deep breath," Arrow said. "Breathing is so important."

The call box had a pin pad with a few little buttons and a small speaker. I pressed the button that said *call* and we waited while a tinny dial tone turned into a phone ringing a million miles away, like it was underwater.

I wanted to turn and run. I wanted to run out of Austin and into Oklahoma; I felt sure that today was the day I would finally figure out how to do it, how to put one foot in front of the other without falling or losing my breath or ending up miles behind. I wanted to run and run and run, but just then the speaker made a little spitting noise and someone who sounded tired and a little sad said, "How can I help you?"

"Hi!" Arrow said when it became clear I wasn't going to say anything. "We're sorry to bother you. We just need a few minutes of your time. For, um, something that can't really be said to a speaker. It's more of a face-to-face thing."

It was Wallace Green. The speaker was slightly garbled and distorted his voice a little, but it was definitely Wallace Green who had answered the phone.

"I'm sorry, sweetheart, this isn't the best time. This is my personal residence, you see, and as much as I appreciate fans of my work I must ask you—"

"YOU'RE MY DAD," I yelled without meaning to.

I had opened my mouth prepared to say something calm and even, and there it was. An awkward scream. Arrow clutched her ear and moaned.

"I'm sorry?" Wallace Green said.

"I think you're my dad. Sir. My mom told me you're my dad. Um, maybe we could come in? Just for a minute? I promise we're not fans. Wait, I mean, I think you're fine. You're a good actor, you know? But you might also be my dad, which is why we're here."

"So smooth," Arrow whispered. "This is the exact approach I'll take if I ever decide to track down my birth parents."

There was a click from the speaker, like Wallace Green had hung up his phone, and my heart fell a little before I realized the gate was buzzing. He was unlocking it for us.

Arrow lunged for the handle and pulled the gate open, and we slipped inside quickly.

"I did not expect that," she said.

"Me neither."

"What do we do now?"

"I guess we follow this path," I said.

"The path to your destiny," Arrow said, and sighed. She looped her arm through mine, and we walked together on the path that followed the driveway through pristinely manicured lawns to a house that looked a little bit like it had been plucked from a fairy tale and set down carefully in our world. It wasn't overly big but it was beautiful and majestic and it made the nervous feeling in my stomach return so suddenly that I stopped walking and clutched my arms around myself, spilling half my coffee in the process. And that's when I noticed the paper coffee cup said *Sally's Diner, best coffee in LA*, and that is when I decided I was probably going to puke, so I dropped the cup and put my hands on my knees and bent over, taking deep breaths that I wasn't entirely sure were actually reaching my lungs.

"Well, this is maybe the strangest story I've heard yet," Wallace Green said, suddenly there before us, standing in the middle of the path.

Arrow squeaked, but I didn't look up until my stomach felt a little more settled, and then I straightened and saw him, in khaki shorts and a short-sleeved T-shirt, his forehead wrinkled as he looked at me closely. "Are you okay, sweetheart?" he said.

"I'm okay," I said.

"I pretty much only let you in because this is the most clever story I've heard so far," he said, not unkindly. "I thought you wanted an autograph, but now I'm a little confused."

"I don't want your autograph," I said. "I think you might be my father."

"And what makes you say that?" he asked, like he was still humoring us, like he still thought we were two fans who might want to take a photo with him, get an autograph, potentially take a tour around his fairy-tale house.

"Look—my mother just died. And before that she was committed to a mental hospital—"

"Wellness center," Arrow clarified.

"Right, except I didn't know that. I thought she moved to Florida. But she was really in this wellness center, and she wrote me all these letters and they were all about how you were my father. And I'm not sure I believe her. . . . I mean, it's probably pointless, me coming here. But she asked me to find you. She wanted me to find you, and I couldn't just ignore that."

As I talked, I grew increasingly aware of how insane everything that came out of my mouth sounded. It was obvious to me now that this man in front of me wasn't my father. He was perfectly nice, perfectly reasonable to assume we were crazed fans, and perfectly right to call the cops and have us removed from his property. Maybe he already had. Maybe they were on their way.

"Arrow, let's go," I said, grabbing her arm quickly and attempting to pull her back toward the front gate.

"Frannie, what are you doing?" she hissed.

"This was a mistake. This whole thing was a mistake. We have to go. I'm sorry, Mr. Green, this was a mistake. Please call the cops back and tell them not to arrest us," I said.

"I didn't call the cops," he said, confused, jogging after us. "Hey, wait a second! Frannie? Is that your name?"

Arrow yanked on my hand, stopping me so suddenly I almost tripped.

"Frances," I said, turning.

"Okay, Frances, you seem like you're telling the truth. I believe you, that your mother told you all that. And what I have to say in response to that is . . . And you might not know this, okay, and it's not because I'm ashamed of anything, it's just because we unfortunately live in a world where not everyone is accepted for who they are. . . ."

"Oh my gosh," Arrow said.

"What?" I said.

"The hole in your mother's story is that . . . I've never been with a woman," Wallace Green finished. "So I can't be your father. I'm sorry."

I stared at him, confused, my ears hot and ringing.

"I'm sorry you came all this way, just to . . . I'm just sorry. It's not possible. I'm gay."

"Oh," I said. "Oh. Okay."

My ears burned hotter, and the ringing replaced the sounds of the real world. I couldn't hear Wallace Green anymore and I couldn't hear Arrow, I could only hear my mother's voice inside my skull, but she wasn't making any sense because my mother was actually, truly crazy. My mother was insane. Why had I ever believed anything my mother told me?

My grandparents were right to keep her from me. They

had made the right decision. Even with them protecting me, she had still sent me on a wild-goose chase to Austin to find a man who—obviously, of course—wasn't my father. Imagine what she would have done if she had still been in my life. Imagine how much worse it could have been.

But still—she was my mother. And now she was really, really gone. There was nothing left to tie her to me or to this world. My real father, Frances the First, was long, long gone. This man standing before me wasn't anybody. Or at least, he wasn't anybody who could bring my mother back.

"I'm so sorry we bothered you," I said. My voice sounded distant and forced. Like it didn't belong to me. An unrecognizable thing.

"It's no bother," Wallace Green said. "It's no bother at all. I'm so sorry. I wish I had something better to tell you."

It only made it worse that Wallace Green was exactly what they said he was. He was unfailingly nice, a Southern gentleman with a subtle accent and horses and a cowboy hat hung up on a peg in his closet. I wanted him to yell. I wanted him to tell me I better get off his property, or else. I half wanted him to call the police because at least the sirens would cut through this awful, awful silence that was building up between us.

"You're not the one who has to be sorry," I said finally, struggling to pull myself together, to just make it through the next few seconds until I could get to the car and fall apart. "It's me. I'm sorry. I'm sorry to have bothered you. We're leaving. Bye."

I didn't wait for him to respond or object or yell or laugh, I just took Arrow's hand and we walked quickly and without looking back. And when we got to my car, I slid into the passenger's seat and let her drive while I put my face in my hands and cried. Not because Wallace Green wasn't my father, because I couldn't care less about that, but because the one thing my mother chose to communicate to me in the last five years of her life, the one thing she found the most important, wasn't even true. That was the biggest loss of all because it meant my mother was crazy. My mother was crazy, and I wasn't far behind.

TWENTY-EIGHT
Louis

That night Willa stayed home again, and I realized it wasn't fatigue, it was a favor. Or, I mean, it was probably some combination of both, because Willa was always tired and she also hated meeting new people and she also, I thought, wanted to give me time alone with Frances.

"Go get 'em, brother," she said halfheartedly, punching me on my shoulder.

"What am I supposed to get?" I asked.

"Oh, you know. Love or whatever," she replied.

"Love or whatever. Noted."

Frances showed up ten minutes late and alone, pulling into the parking lot of Holdem just a little too quickly and parking crooked in a spot as far away from the restaurant as she could get. I met her at her car. She looked frazzled and upset and like maybe she had been crying. At least—her eyes were rimmed in red and her face looked raw and wiped clean.

"I'm sorry," she said. "I'm sorry I'm late."

"It's fine. It's totally fine. Are you okay? You don't look . . ."

I didn't want to imply that she didn't look good so I second-guessed myself and let the sentence slide into the negative space of unfinished thoughts. I reached out and took her hand without really thinking about it, and she launched herself in my arms like a spaceship. And I was the universe, or something. I wasn't really thinking clearly.

She pressed her face against my T-shirt and I thought she was going to cry again, but she just kind of held on tightly for a few seconds and then let go suddenly, pulling away with a smile on her face, a strange smile that looked okay in the twilight but was probably not really okay at all.

"It didn't go well, did it?" I asked.

"Ugh, the opposite of well. It was a disaster. It was really the stuff of nightmares," she confirmed, almost laughing.

"I'm sorry."

"I guess I thought this would fix things." She sat down and leaned against one of her car's tires. I knelt down across from her. "Now I don't even know why I came here."

"Oh," I said, before I could stop myself.

She looked up quickly and put her hand on my knee. "Oh, I'm sorry," she said. "That was terrible."

"I know what you mean."

"I didn't mean you, Louis. Of course I didn't mean you. That came out wrong."

"I know."

"I mean . . . if I didn't have you, if I didn't have this . . ." She shook her head, trailing off. "All I meant was, I came all this way to prove to myself that my mother wasn't completely gone. Like somehow, in my head, if I proved that Wallace Green was actually my father, then there would be something on this earth that she had left me. I don't know if that makes any sense."

"It makes sense. I'm sorry it didn't work out."

"It's okay. I don't think I want to talk about Wallace Green right now. Or maybe I do, you know, but not in this parking lot. Or maybe I don't. Did you know he was gay?"

"Really? No. I've never heard that."

"So he can't be my father."

"I'm sorry, Frannie."

"That's fine. I mean, it was never really about him. It was never really about Wallace Green." She paused, stood up, leaned against her car, smiled again. She had more smiles than anyone I'd ever met before. I wanted to know what each of them meant. "She was so adamant. In all her letters, she was so adamant. I wanted to believe her for her sake, maybe. Because she seemed so sure. I don't know why she was so obsessed with it, but it was almost like the only thing she had left. Maybe because she thought nobody would ever be able to disprove it." Frannie held her arms out, laughed quietly. "She must not have really known me. I'll disprove anything."

Frannie stepped away from her car and grabbed my hand. "I'm sorry. I don't mean to throw all this at you."

"It's okay. You can talk to me about anything."

It was true but it also felt somehow not enough, it somehow fell short of the grand gesture I wanted it to be. It needed to be bigger. I could rent a skywriter and paste it across the clouds: *You can tell me anything.* I could name a star after her or write it out in something valuable, like gold or diamonds. I just wanted her to know that I meant it, and words didn't seem big enough to convey that. Or maybe I didn't feel big enough to convey that. Whatever it was, it was breaking my heart that she looked so sad, that she had come so far and hadn't found what she wanted to find.

Maybe I just wanted to be what she wanted to find.

That might have been the most selfish thing I'd ever admitted to myself.

"I'm not really hungry anymore," she said after a while, after a silence that seemed impossibly expansive to me, built up and heavy with meaning.

"Me neither," I said.

"Gosh, are we terrible at dates? We're terrible at dates. I think it just feels too hot to eat anything."

"Walk?" I said, trying to keep my brain from repeating her word choice over and over and over: *date date date*. I knew it wasn't the most important word she had just said, but I couldn't help it.

She put her hand into mine, and we left the parking lot of Holdem, retracing our same steps of the night before. Except the night before we hadn't held hands, but it seemed like a natural progression.

Frannie was quiet for a long time, so I stayed quiet for a long time because I didn't want to break the fragile air between us. I wanted to be whatever she wanted me to be, and I think at that moment she wanted me to be silent.

We walked until we came to the river that sliced through the city. Frannie pointed out a little sign that said Shoal Beach, and we found a bench and sat with our hips touching. Frannie held her hands on her lap, and I wanted to reach for one but there were too many entwined fingers. It felt like a trap. I wouldn't know where to start. And then I wanted to put my arm around her shoulders but that felt too much like a high school movie theater date, so I folded my hands like hers and kept my arms to myself.

"It's pretty here," she said. The first words spoken since we'd left the Holdem parking lot.

"It wasn't what I was expecting."

"Me neither. Or, I dunno. I don't know what I was expecting."

"Was he nice?"

"Wallace Green?"

"Yeah. I mean, was he a dick?"

"No, he wasn't a dick. He seemed . . . Well, he almost seemed disappointed he couldn't help me more. But it's not his fault, you know?"

"I'm glad he wasn't a dick."

"He seemed nice. Everything you read about him says he's nice too."

I didn't know what to say so I said, "It wasn't a waste. Coming here."

"I guess I've always wanted to do a road trip."

"Well, sure. I also meant . . ."

I knew what I wanted to say. *I also meant us, together. The Colorado River before us. The stars and moon and black-blue sky above us. My hand in your hand. Skipping dinner and walking until my blisters don't even hurt anymore, because they're too numb. The soles of my shoes black and worn smooth. The smell of the city—something like fire or smoke or the sharp tinge of sulfur.*

Frannie reached over and squeezed my hand, and then she squeezed my fingers one by one, almost methodically, like she was working some kind of strange braille on my skin. But it was too complicated to follow, and I lost her message somewhere between my middle and ring fingers.

She stood up and took a few steps toward the water, resting her forearms on a low wooden fence. I put my hand on the bench to push myself up to join her, and I felt something underneath my fingers. I picked up a thick photograph from an old instant camera. The white borders were yellowed and wrinkled but the image was clear. A woman, laughing, being led out of frame by someone wearing a thick bracelet, silver with a blue stone.

Frannie had once told me she didn't look anything like her father, either the nonfamous or the famous one, that she looked exactly like her mother, as if she were conceived and birthed without the help of any Y chromosomes. I could see it in this picture. I knew this wasn't Frances—the clothes and hairstyle were indicative of another decade—but it could be her in costume. This woman's laugh was Frannie's laugh; her smile was Frannie's smile; her eyes were Frannie's eyes.

I stood up and went to stand next to Frances, handing her the photo.

"Your mom looked really happy," I said, because Willa always yelled at me if "beautiful" was the first thing I commented on. But Frances's mom was beautiful too, because Frances was beautiful and because they looked like they could be twins.

"She never looked this happy in real life," Frances said, taking the photo and holding it up to catch the glow of the streetlight behind us. She didn't ask me where the photo had come from, maybe because we had both accepted something was going on that was without explanation, and we'd decided just to allow it to run its course.

"This *was* real life," I said. "Just a moment of it, maybe, but still."

"By the time the photograph was developed, she was probably already scowling," Frannie argued.

"But you never have to know that. There's no proof. Just let her be happy."

"Louis, you are something I've never encountered before," she said, slipping the photo into her pocket and turning to face me.

"I like you too," I said.

We stayed by the river for hours.

TWENTY-NINE
Frances

I think we might have stayed by the river forever if we hadn't skipped dinner two nights in a row. We were both starving, and so Louis pulled out his phone and found a place that served tacos. And neither of us wanted to go back to Holdem because (I imagined, I hoped) that meant being close to our cars, which meant being close to leaving. And I didn't want to leave. I didn't want this night to end, because I didn't think we would get a second chance. We lived so far away from each other. I just didn't think it was possible.

We walked with the river on our right. It was past nine

o'clock, and the city was filled with a purple sort of moonlight that reflected off the water and made the world seem like it was born in a fantasy novel. I tried to commit everything to memory, to make everything last, but even as we walked it was slipping away. But maybe the best things were always meant to fade into fuzzy memory. Maybe that's what made them special.

"I don't know what I should do," Louis said after a few minutes.

"About what?"

"About anything."

"Me neither. You said once that maybe there are parallel-universe versions of ourselves. I wish we could hire them to make decisions for us."

"There's no way of telling if they'd actually be smarter than these versions of us," he pointed out, smiling. "They might do really stupid things."

"Would you even care? At this point I feel like I need to put all these options into a hat and then just go with whatever I pull out first."

"That sounds like a terrible idea," he said, laughing now. He reached for my hand and squeezed it. Then I squeezed even harder, so he couldn't let go.

"What are you thinking about?" I asked. "The university?"

"Yeah, I'm kind of constantly thinking about it. The

tour was nice, you know? Is that a weird word to use to describe it?"

"I don't know. I think nice is a nice word."

"It was nice. It felt . . . I guess it didn't feel as overwhelming as I thought it would feel. It felt kind of natural."

"Like it fit?"

"Like it fit, yeah. And I saw the tennis courts, and those were great. And the whole place is really beautiful. It wasn't like I had imagined."

"It sounds like you've made up your mind?" I asked.

"I don't know," he said. "Maybe. I keep practicing in my head what I would tell Willa and my parents. Sometimes it goes well, sometimes my mother starts crying immediately."

"You really don't think she'd want you to go here?"

"I know she'd want to be supportive, but I think she also has this dream that Willa and I will live in Los Angeles forever, preferably taking over the family business and living in our apartment until we both die. On the same day."

"That's intense."

"Or who knows. Maybe she'd be proud."

"I'm sure she's already proud of you." I wanted to say more, like *it must be nice to have a mother who didn't slowly spiral out of control. It must be nice to have a father who didn't stab you when you were just a kid. It must be nice to have a nuclear family. I think those are overrated, and I'm jealous of you and yours.* "And I'm sure she'll support whatever you decide to do," I added.

"Maybe that's it—that this is kind of the first thing we really have to decide, you know? Going to college is this huge choice, and it's so hard to figure out if you're making the right one. You can do research, tour schools, look at course books . . . but it still feels so random. Like you said, picking a choice out of a hat."

"But it's easier for you. They came to you."

"That's only another level of confusion. Do I want to go here because I want to go here or do I want to go here because it's easy? Because there's no risk, they've already told me I'll get in."

"I'd take that option any day," I said.

We'd reached the taco stand, which was really just a glorified food truck with a few picnic tables strewn out front. A woman in red cowboy boots was sharing a beer with a friend, another table was crowded with college students stuffing queso and chips into their mouths and discussing whether they thought the owner would card them if they tried to buy beer.

I saved us a table while Louis went and ordered guacamole and grilled corn with chili pepper and cheese and lime and tacos stuffed with cactus, cheese dripping out of the sides.

"I didn't know you could eat cactus," he said, setting

everything down on the table.

"Was it the weirdest thing on the menu? My grandpa always says if you eat somewhere new, you should order the weirdest thing on the menu."

"The weirdest thing on the menu was definitely the tongue taco," he said. "But cactus was the weirdest thing that I would actually eat."

He laughed and slid onto the bench. We each grabbed a taco and clinked them together like they were drinks. Then, the cheese sliding down our knuckles, we took our first bites.

"It's good!" Louis said.

"It's very cheesy."

"That's probably why it's good."

I scooped up a small mountain of guacamole on a chip and ate it. It put all previous guacamole to shame. All the guacamole of my lifetime was a pale imitation of this treasure in front of me.

"Wow," I said.

"The East Coast doesn't have good avocadoes," Louis said, trying some. "This is really good."

"Have you ever been to the East Coast? We have better seafood, I guess. But I don't eat seafood."

"I've never been. And I'm allergic to fish. Have you been to California?"

"When I was little, with my mom. We used to drive all over the place. Everything kind of blended together."

"Have you been here before?"

"Texas, yes. But I don't know if we came to Austin."

"I thought there'd be more cowboy hats."

"She's wearing cowboy boots," I said, pointing to the woman who was now cleaning up her picnic table.

"I guess that's something."

I finished my taco and took a bite of the corn, which of course immediately stuck in between every one of my teeth. Louis handed me a toothpick wrapped in plastic that he'd gotten with the forks.

We ate our corn and finished the guacamole and when the paper plates were empty, we were quiet because everything felt so close to being over. Louis got up and threw everything out, and I went and stood by the sidewalk. When he joined me he said, "What's wrong?"

And I said, "We're running out of time."

"Time for what?"

"For everything. Here. High school. Teenage years."

"I know," he said quietly, and took my hand.

Then I didn't know what to say. I didn't know anything except the fact that I didn't want this night to end. I wanted to find a way to bottle it up, to take it home with me and keep it on my bureau, one of those ships that fold in on themselves so you can slip them into their new glass home and then expand them again so they're full and big and so they can't escape. I wanted this night to be my very own ship in a bottle. I wanted to keep it forever on paper waves, lit by moonlight and drawn in yellow paint.

"Let's stay up all night," I said without meaning to say it. Then I closed my eyes and looked away from him because I didn't think I could bear it if he said no.

THIRTY
Louis

"That's exactly what I was going to say," I answered.
"Really?" she asked, looking over me at hopefully.

I took her hand and squeezed it and then I had to look down and see our two hands together because it was almost too hard to believe: I was holding Frannie's hand and I had just eaten cactus tacos with her in a city we had never been to before and now we were trying to figure out a way to make time stand still because sometimes the world was too confusing to keep up with and you just needed more time to figure everything out.

"Really," I said.

"What should we do?" she asked. "Where should we go?"

"Whatever. Wherever."

She pulled me down the sidewalk, away from the taco stand and away from the main buzz of the city and back to the path along the water. There were less people here, and although it was hot, there was a slight breeze off the water.

"Do you know what you'll do? After high school?" I asked, because I realized that we'd talked about the University of Texas but I had no idea what Frannie's plans were.

"I don't know," she said. "My mom spent time abroad. I think I'd like to do that."

"Where?"

"In England. I've never been out of the United States."

"I've just been to India."

"Oh, just?" she said, laughing.

"Well I mean, I'd like to go someplace else too. I'd like to travel."

"I guess that's a good thing. About the future, you know. We can do more of what we want to do. We're almost adults."

"I don't really feel like an adult."

"Me neither," she said. "I think sometimes people—grown-ups—they put all this pressure on us to figure out every single step of our lives, every single connected dot, but in reality people are figuring things out as they go." She pulled the picture of her mother out of her pocket. "Like my mom," she said. "I used to think she had a plan, but really she was just trying to hold on for as long as she could."

"When do think that was taken?" I asked.

"I thought it was taken about nine months before I was born," she replied, her voice darkening a little. We paused underneath a streetlight, and she held the picture higher so we both could see it.

"And now?" I asked.

"Now I have absolutely no idea. I'm not even sure if it matters anymore. It's just a moment now. A meaningless moment."

"My mother would say that no moments are meaningless," I said, and then I felt weird, like maybe I shouldn't have brought her up. She could be overbearing and oppressive and constantly present, but at least she was here. At least she was my mother, someone who constantly texted me to check in and was never dissuaded when I didn't respond (she'd sent me fourteen texts already that day, texts filled with emojis of sun and palm trees and an egg frying on a skillet next to a blue car—I think that was supposed to mean it was really hot in Los Angeles), and at least she had never left me. I couldn't imagine what it must feel like to be Frannie. To not have parents.

"Your mother sounds very optimistic," Frannie said.

"I think she means that you can find meaning in any-thing. Or you can find the meaninglessness in everything. It goes both ways."

"Isn't that kind of like cheating?"

"Yeah, but life is kind of like cheating."

Frannie smiled and put her hand on my arm. "I like you, Louis. You're different from anyone I've ever met."

She pulled me along the path. I had no idea where we were or where we were going, where our cars were or how to get back to them. I let her lead us until we were away from the river and along a street lined with bars built in small converted houses.

"I read about this place," she said.

We walked along the length of it and at the other end we found a small circle of food trucks. Frannie pulled me to an ice cream truck and bought us two small cups that we ate sitting on the curb, watching people hopping from one house to another like they weren't visiting bars but neighbors and friends.

"Does Willa know where she's going to college?" she asked.

"Some Ivy League, probably."

"Wow."

"Yeah, she's always been the smarter one. She'll end up a doctor or something. What about Arrow?"

"She wants to go to Boston or New York. Maybe I'll go with her, I don't know. It would be nice to have someone I know there."

"That would be fun. I've never really been in the cold before. Los Angeles, India . . . now Texas. It seems to be hot wherever I go."

"You should visit Maryland in the winter," she said quietly, and I couldn't tell if that was just something to say or something more, like an invitation. But that was stupid. Didn't we both know this was Austin and nothing further? Or maybe it didn't have to be. I didn't know anymore. The moonlight was confusing everything. The purple light was making everything more beautiful than it already was. Including Frannie, who had finished her ice cream and gone to throw it away in a trash can under the flickering streetlight, who pulled away and spun out into the night—spinning, spinning until she started laughing. She leaned up against the next streetlight to steady herself. Up top, near the bulb, a hundred insects swarmed and buzzed. The air around us vibrated as I threw away my ice cream cup and then stopped in front of her and this time took both her hands in both of mine.

"Are you better now?" she asked.

"What do you mean?"

"You know," she said, and touched my forearm.

That wasn't where any of the scars were, but I recoiled a little anyway. I had told her about it, of course. I had told

Frannie everything that had ever happened to me, over years and years and behind the safety of a computer screen. But this—being in front of her—this was something new.

"I don't think so," I said finally, and it felt like a secret. It felt like something I knew but couldn't admit until now.

No, it wasn't better.

No, it had never gotten better.

I was just better at hiding it. I was better at postponing it. I was tired of therapy and tired of feeling like Willa was the unlucky one but somehow, somehow the more stable one. I was tired of everything. I didn't know what else I could do.

"What does it feel like?" she asked.

"Like I have no other option."

"But you do. You know that, right?"

"Sometimes I can't see it," I said.

She bit her bottom lip and looked away. "I think we need to close our accounts."

"TILT?"

"This Is Losing Time," she said.

"This Is Lovelier, Though."

"I don't know, it just feels like the right thing to do. I mean, it's always felt like a weird kind of crutch. I don't even do the sessions anymore. I was really just keeping it so I could talk to you."

"I think I've kept it around so long just in case I need

it. But I don't need it anymore. I think I need something different now."

"Different how?"

"I'm not sure. Maybe something . . . more real."

"We'll still have each other," she said softly, pulling me just a little closer toward her.

"I know."

"Even if we're still far away."

"I know."

"Like even if—"

"I know," I said again, and then leaned forward slowly, slowly enough that she could push me away if she wanted to, slowly enough that I could change my mind if I decided it was the stupidest thing I'd ever done, slowly, slowly, slowly. . . . The distance between two things so phenomenally far apart from each other crossed at the slowest possible rate. And when they collided, there was only buzzing and humming and the bone-deep vibration of a thousand light-seeking beasts. Which might have been gross, I guess, if we had looked up. But we didn't look up. We were seeking our own light, and we had just found it.

THIRTY-ONE
Frances

Arrow and I packed up the motel room in silence early the next morning. The trip to Austin, the excitement from a few days ago, everything within us—it all felt deflated. Last night with Louis had been quiet and nice and wonderful and we'd done what we said we'd do, we'd stayed up all night, and I'd crawled into bed as dawn was stretching out over the city and the second I closed my eyes, pretending I'd be able to sleep, I felt whatever had been building up between us burst. Like a balloon going into the sky. Up and up and up and it looks so peaceful and pretty from the ground but up there, up where the balloon floats, the pressure becomes too much. It explodes. All of the air leaks out of it. It falls back to earth and becomes just another thing littered on the sidewalk. Just another thing to pick up and throw away or else ignore and step on.

Arrow woke up when I got back. She rolled over, and we faced each other in the darkness. The blinds were pulled tightly over the windows and it was dark in the room; I could barely see her eyes, two white circles floating in space.

"Hi," she whispered.

"Hi."

"How was it?"

"It was perfect," I said. "It was terrible. It was horrible."

"Because it can never be," Arrow guessed.

"Yeah, because of that."

"There is something to be said for distance."

"That it sucks?"

"That it sucks, yes. But that it is also sometimes romantic and good."

"Romantic and good," I echoed. "What else do they say?"

"They say everything looks better in the morning."

"It *is* the morning."

"They say everything looks better in the afternoon."

"Or else everything looks worse."

"They say no matter what things look like in the afternoon, a change of perspective is sometimes the best thing for it."

"Arrow, thanks for coming with me."

"I didn't come with you. We went together. Forth into the great unknown like two modern-day adventurers, et cetera, et cetera."

"What would I do without you?"

"You would have come alone, I expect. Don't sell yourself short. Now if you don't mind, I was in the middle of a very nice dream, and I'm going to try to get back to it."

She fell asleep again for an hour or two, and I stayed awake flicking through pictures in my phone: a pair of black bean tacos, a blurry selfie of the two of us, the orange and pink of the sky just before dawn when we finally made it back to our cars.

"Why do I feel like I'll never sleep again?" I had said, smiling up at him and the lightening sky above his head.

"Let's run away together," he had whispered into my ear, touching me gently on my right hip, just the lightest breeze before he moved his hand away again.

And I had whispered back, "We already have."

Now Arrow was carefully rolling her shirts into neat cylinders (they didn't wrinkle as much that way, she claimed) and stacking them into her suitcase with delicate precision. When she noticed me watching her, she stopped and straightened up.

"What was your dream about?" I asked, struggling to pull myself out of a daydream that didn't seem like it could have been real.

She grinned at me. "The best dreams are not fit for public consumption."

"I'm not the public."

"That's a fair point. I guess I'll tell you, only if you promise to tell me everything that happened between you and Louis. No more of this secretive stuff."

"Okay, I promise."

"Give me something to work with. Consider it a down payment."

"Well . . . ," I started. I was going to tell her about the kiss beneath the streetlight but apparently she had already guessed it. She covered her face with her hands and squealed.

"Oh, I knew it," she said. "I knew it. Was it nice?"

"Of course it was nice! It was the nicest."

"Nicer than anything?"

"Nicer than most things, yes. Now what was your dream about?"

"Returning a certain handkerchief to its rightful owner."

"Hank Whitney?" I guessed.

"Indeed. But until then, let me treat you to breakfast."

"Because you want to go back to the weird knitting diner?"

"You know me so well, it's like I don't even have to speak."

She finished packing her suitcase. I walked from the bedroom to the bathroom under the guise of making sure I hadn't left anything behind, but really I just felt like walking and didn't have many options. I was ready to leave Austin, and, having decided that, I wanted to be gone. I didn't want to wait any longer. I wanted to pull the Band-Aid off with one fluid yank.

But I knew it wasn't that simple. I found my phone in my purse and sent a text to Louis with the name and address of the restaurant.

Meet us here if you can. Would love to say good-bye.

That was a lie, of course. I wouldn't love to say good-bye. Not in the slightest. But I didn't think I'd be able to forgive myself if I didn't.

Arrow and I sat in the back of the station wagon, the hatchback shading us from the late morning sun, our feet dangling and swinging, my hands folded in my lap and gripping each other like they might fly away if I didn't hold them tight enough.

"I can't believe you stayed up all night," Arrow said. I had told her everything, of course, or as much as I could in the car ride from the motel to the diner. "It's like a fairy tale, Frannie. You're like a princess. You're Cinderella!"

"Cinderella only stayed out until midnight."

"Right, but you know that girl would have kept dancing if her carriage didn't turn back into a pumpkin."

Louis and Willa were on time; we were early. I watched their car pull into the parking lot, and I watched Louis get out first and wait around the back until Willa had emerged from the passenger seat. He said something to her that I couldn't hear, and she shook her head, smiling. Her smile took effort. It wasn't easy. But then it turned wider and more real and she squeezed her brother's elbow and laughed once. He pointed over at us, and they started walking together.

Willa wore a knee-length skirt and tennis shoes. She walked fluidly and I tried to imagine, if I couldn't see her prosthetic legs, if I didn't already know the exact spot on her thighs where her real legs ended, if I would have been able to tell. I don't think I would have, if only because her face provided such an immediate distraction. She was absolutely beautiful, makeupless and sleepy and slightly scowling. Even when she smiled she had lines in her face. I wanted to hug her because she looked at once so much like Louis but somehow also like she could be a perfect stranger.

"Hi," she said, waving her hand at hip level when she was close enough to talk to us. "I'm Willa."

"Willa, this is Frances," Louis said. "You must be

Arrow. I've heard so much about you." He shook Arrow's hand. We finished introductions and stood in silence in the parking lot, not awkwardly but somehow at ease. I'd spent a lot of time in parking lots the past few days.

Louis spoke first. It took me too long to process his words and he had to repeat them, blushing—he blushed so easily—raising his voice to call the group to attention. "Should we go inside?" he asked.

"I'm starving," Willa said.

"I'm so hungry," Arrow agreed. They walked together across the parking lot, and Louis and I followed. I thought he might take my hand and I couldn't decide whether I wanted him to or not, but then he did and I thought—*Of course. Of course I want you to. It's just that in a few hours I will want you to again, but you won't be here. I'll be on my way to Maryland and you'll be on your way to California and you can't really get two people farther away than that. The miles stack up on top of each other, and even if Arrow was right, even if distance is romantic, it is also impossible. It is too much to fathom. It is too much to overcome.*

He let go of my hand when we got to the restaurant door, but he put his palm on my back and let me go in front of him. We sat down at a booth and our same waitress brought over mugs of coffee but didn't seem like she recognized us.

"It's so nice to finally meet you," Willa said to us, and even though she wasn't smiling, it felt like such an honest thing to say. She just shrugged and said it. And we started talking about Austin and our separate coastal towns and I watched a clock with golden retriever puppies count down the minutes much too quickly. It had to be broken. Somebody should fix it; somebody should put time in its proper place or else the whole world would end before we even left this table.

I wished we'd never leave this table.

But our pancakes came and our eggs came and our coffee cups were refilled, and Willa told a hysterical story of Louis as a preteen refusing to let go of his belief in Santa Claus. And then we had finished our food and the plates were cleared away, and we'd all drank too much coffee and paid our bill with jittery, messy hands. We stood in the parking lot for too long. I didn't think we wanted to say good-bye because something had clicked into place and nobody wanted to be responsible for disassembling it.

Finally it was Arrow.

Sometimes I thought she was the best at good-byes because she had been taught at such an early age that they were unavoidable and it was worthless to try to prolong them. But probably it was just because she knew I couldn't make myself say the words, and she always did what I couldn't do. And vice versa.

"It was so nice to meet you both," Arrow said. "I know I'll see you again."

She hugged Willa and Louis and then Willa hugged me

and kissed my cheek and then it was only Louis and me. He put the back of his hand against my cheek, and it felt so good I wanted to cry. But I didn't cry. I hugged him.

"It was so nice to see your face," I said.

"You have the nicest face of anybody I've ever met," he replied.

"We'll keep in touch, of course."

"You make it sound like we're leaving summer camp."

"Wear the friendship bracelet I made you, okay?"

"I'm sorry the lake water gave you a gastrointestinal infection."

"We'll always have the campfires."

"Kumbaya," he said. "I really like you, Frannie."

"I really like you, Louis."

"I tried to close my TILT account on my phone," he said. "But the app signed me out, and I've never been very good with passwords."

"Bucker is now my password," I said automatically. It just appeared in my brain, one more thing he'd lost and I'd found, one more thing I could give to him. I wanted to give him everything. He put his hand on the back of my neck, and I thought he was going to kiss me but he only hugged me, so tightly I almost lost my breath.

"You're amazing," he whispered in my hair. "And you smell like pancakes."

I wrapped my arms around his shoulders and said, "It was all worth it. Every mile."

When he pulled away, minutes later, I could still feel him.

When I drove out of the parking lot, I could still feel him.

All the way back home, I could still feel him. It was like he had never left.

THIRTY-TWO
Louis

The car felt smaller on the way home. And hotter—like the heat of Austin had gotten trapped in the fabric of the seats, the fake leather detailing, the steering wheel, the rearview mirrors. Willa didn't complain but tilted the vents to blow cold air on her face. Her hair whipped around her until eventually she put it into a ponytail.

"I don't want to stop along the way," she said when we passed the city limits and left Austin behind us, a memory in the span of an instant.

I didn't mention that I'd already been up for twenty-four hours (Willa hadn't woken up when I'd gotten back to the motel room that morning) because, to be honest, I wasn't tired at all. I felt awake in a way I hadn't in years—a healthy, natural awake. Like I had woken up from a two-hour nap on the heels of a full eight-hour night of sleep. I knew I could drive to Los Angeles just like I knew that when we got there, finally, I might be ready for some sleep.

I drove away from Austin and my sister fiddled with the air vents and I felt the passing of time like it was a physical thing. Like every minute was slipping through my fingers, every hour was ripping itself out of my chest and taking part of me with it.

When I was younger, I would get panic attacks if I watched a clock for too long. It never seemed fair that we were only given one opportunity, one chance, and that even in the second we completed a task it was already behind us. We could never reach it again. We could never test whether it had been the right decision or not. We could only pick a direction—left or right—and commit to it blindly, jumping off into the proverbial deep end. Sometimes it was nice, cool water. Sometimes it was shit.

It had helped when I cut myself.

I'd started after Willa's accident, and I'd relished the release I felt.

But it was a fake release, I knew. It was something I'd made up in my head to prolong the inevitability of facing my problems. I'd worked through it in therapy, and I knew now that I had to go back. When I told Frannie I thought

I needed something more, I meant—no more TILTgroup, no more half-assed group therapy sessions on the internet. I had to go back to real-life, one-on-one sessions. I had to tell Dr. Williams that I had wanted to hurt myself again. I had to tell her the urge had come back in a motel room in the middle of nowhere and I had come really close to losing that battle. I had to tell her that I had no idea why it had happened when it happened. Maybe it was random. Maybe it was being so far from home. Maybe it was the fact that for the first time in my life I had stopped focusing on all the things I was losing, and I was starting to go out and find the things I wanted for myself.

Willa was watching me. I saw her out of the corner of my eye.

"It's a twenty-hour drive," I said.

"We can go to a drive-thru if we get hungry."

"I mean, I'll have to pee."

"Well, obviously we can pee. I just want to sleep in my own bed, Louis."

It was one in the afternoon. We would arrive in Los Angeles around eleven in the morning the next day.

"I guess we can try," I said, but I already knew I could make it. Willa would fall asleep and wake up a dozen times, napping her way to Los Angeles, and I would drive and drive and drive until we got home.

"That's your problem, Louis," she said, forcing her words through a yawn. "You can never commit."

"Speaking of commitment, what are you going to do about Benson?"

She straightened up in her seat, stretching her hands out in front of her before answering. "Are you asking me whether I'm ready to lose my virginity?"

"In as many words."

"Well it's not really any of your business."

"To be fair, you're the one who brought it up."

"You tricked me. And anyway, I don't know."

"You don't have to know right now."

"What are you, a psychologist? Geez."

"I'm just trying to fill up our twenty-hour drive with some conversation."

"Let's fill it with naptime. Not for you, though. You have to watch the road."

I drove for six hours before my legs started tingling. Willa slept for two and then woke up and mostly alternated between changing the music and staring out the window despondently. I didn't know what she had to be despondent about. She and Benson lived in the same city. She had a choice that I didn't have.

Every minute of the six hours was filled with Frances.

We had gotten to know each other over the course of years. She had told me everything about her life, so much that before I saw her picture I knew what she looked like, and before I talked to her on the phone I knew what she sounded like, and before I ever touched her I knew what she would feel like. So many times in those six hours I wanted to slam my foot on the brake, turn around, drive to wherever she was, and take her in my arms again, hug her close to me so she couldn't escape.

But something kept me on the path. On my path. I had to go back to Los Angeles so I could leave it again when it was the right time. I had to tell my parents I was going to Austin after graduation; I had to finish high school and get grades good enough to keep my scholarship. I had to figure out a way to pack up my things and move them halfway across the country. I had to figure out a way to do all of this while knowing that Frances was in the world and I couldn't be with her.

I stopped the car by a restaurant in the middle of nowhere. I liked it because there were cows grazing on the front lawn. Willa had fallen asleep again, and when I turned the car off she jerked awake.

"Where are we?"

"Someplace called Kent. We're still in Texas," I said.

"Oh. I thought we might be home already."

"It would be impressive, even for you, to sleep for twenty hours."

"I was trying," she said. "I'll try harder next time."

We ate a quick dinner and got back on the road. The closer we got to Los Angeles, the quieter Willa became, like the city would only let her back in if she was still. We stopped again around ten at night and stocked up on snacks at a seedy gas station. Willa got bananas and potato chips and an enormous container of unsalted cashews. I got a can of soda for the caffeine, a bag of pretzels, and three apples. We feasted in the parking lot and then snacked the rest of the way to the city, passing into Los Angeles just before noon.

My legs were useless when I finally pulled up next to our apartment building. I rubbed my thighs to get the blood flowing again. Willa reached over and slapped my knee.

"Now you sort of know how I feel, except no amount of rubbing will bring that feeling back," she said. When she said things like that, I didn't know how to respond. I didn't know if maybe saying nothing was my best bet. I was generally really good at saying nothing, except I'd just driven for twenty-one hours and felt a little sentimental for a variety of reasons. So I grabbed her hand before she pulled it away.

"You know when I said I wished it was me? Years ago, I don't remember when. You brushed it off, and I never knew how to tell you that I meant it. I really meant it. I wish it was me. I wish we could switch. Or I wish we could share."

"Like we each had one leg?" she asked, beginning to smile.

"Yeah. I wish I could give you one of my legs. I wish I could share my body with you. Not in a weird way."

"It sounds pretty weird," she said, but now she was smiling widely.

"I mean it so much, though. I think you're the coolest person I've ever met," I continued.

"Louis . . ."

"I'm being serious. And if Benson can't see that, or if you can't see that—if anyone has trouble seeing that from now until the end of our lives, you can give them my number. I will show them the error of their ways."

"Geez, Louis, we should take road trips more often. You've never been this nice to me." But she wasn't smiling anymore. She looked almost sad. I let go of her hand, and she shook her hair out of its ponytail. It had a ridge running through it where the elastic had been. She wrapped her hair around her fingers and then let it go and then took it up again. She looked like she might cry, but I didn't know what she'd be crying about. And I didn't think I'd ever seen my sister cry.

Finally she said, "I was lying too. When I told you I never wished it was you. Because sometimes I did." She took a deep breath. "But I was young and bitter, and I didn't know why this had happened to me. I was too young and bitter to realize that some things happen for no reason at all. Some things hold no meaning. Accidents are accidents, and it doesn't help to continually wish for something different. I will never be able to go back and not crawl onto the fire escape. No matter how much I lied to myself, I will never actually believe it was your idea. It wasn't your fault. It was just a stupid thing. Kids do stupid things. Sometimes they backfire and you're left with no legs forever."

She patted her knees, and I tried to remember them when they were real, flesh and bone. But knees are something you rarely pay attention to. It was hard for me to picture Willa whole. Instead she was in pieces. Removable legs. Torso.

She wrinkled her nose and opened the passenger door. I became aware of how incredibly tired I was, how my eyes were closing even as I struggled to keep them open. I hadn't slept in two days and my systems were shutting down. I got out of the car and used Willa's wheelchair to stack our suitcases so we'd only have to make one trip. I wheeled it in front of me. Willa brought up the rear.

Our apartment smelled like home in the way it only did after such a long time away. I rolled the wheelchair into the kitchen and stumbled into my bedroom, kicking off my sneakers before I threw myself on the covers, almost flattening Bucker, who was curled up on the pillow. He put one paw on the back of my head. When I woke up later to smells of lasagna filling the apartment, he was gone.

I was still tired; my eyes were heavy and dry, but my desire to go back to sleep was trumped by my desire to eat dinner.

Someone had put my suitcase in my bedroom, and I almost tripped on it in the dark. I felt along the wall for the light switch and clicked it on. I put my suitcase on the bed and opened it up. I wanted to put in a load of wash before I ate. I took out dirty clothes and piled them on my floor, then set my tennis racket carefully on my bed (I didn't know if my dad was in the country, but I couldn't wait to show it to him—I would tell him I'd found it in a closet, he would not know whether to believe me and he would shake his head slowly, up and down, many times before he shrugged and decided to let it be) before checking the inside pockets of the suitcase to make sure I hadn't forgotten anything.

One of the pockets had a folded piece of paper in it so I took it out and smoothed it open on my bed. I thought it might be the permission slip from Willa's doctor's office, but this was something else. A bill for something.

A coffin.

The bill came from the Easton Valley Rest and Recuperation Center for the Permanently Unwell.

I wondered what sense they made, these things we lost and then found again. What was the point? What was the correlation? What did my tennis racket and the bill for Frannie's mother's coffin have in common? What did anything have in common? What was the thread that linked everything together?

I crumpled the bill and tossed it into the wastebasket. They would send Frannie another one and another one until her grandparents finally paid the fourteen hundred dollars. You couldn't really lose a bill. It would just keep multiplying forever. There were bigger things to lose. A stack of letters or a pair of sunglasses you really like. A cup of coffee or a phone number—those weren't things to worry about.

My sister stuck her head into the room. "Louis, dinner's ready. Also, you look like a shower wouldn't hurt you."

She left my door open. I joined her and my mom at the table and wondered if it was over now, if I wouldn't lose anything ever again, or if that was too much to hope for.

I ate slowly and when I was done I called Frannie. Her voice sounded far away but it helped if I closed my eyes. I listened to her in the dark.

THIRTY-THREE
Frances

Arrow drove for twelve hours straight. We ate the last of the banana nut bread and spent the night in Nashville, Tennessee. Arrow was so tired she forgot to put her sleeping bag on the bed, and she woke up in the middle of the night from a dream about bedbugs.

"There aren't any bedbugs in Tennessee," I whispered in the darkness.

"You don't know that. You don't know anything about bedbugs."

"I know a lot about bedbugs."

"How do you know so much about bedbugs?"

I didn't know anything about bedbugs, but I did know

how to calm Arrow down, so I told her I'd seen a certificate in the lobby from an exterminator that presented the motel with a clean bill of bug health. I was particularly impressed with that lie. Arrow went back to sleep, and I stayed awake looking at the ceiling and then looking at my phone, turning the brightness down so it wouldn't wake her up again.

Louis hadn't texted me, but I hadn't texted him either. I wondered if he was still finding things I had lost along the way or if maybe that was finally over.

I wondered if maybe everything was over.

And then I wondered if I would ever see him again, and if I did see him again, would it be like it had been in Austin or would it be different? Would we be different?

And then I fell asleep thinking about the way he held my hand and the way I had only known him for days or for years, depending on how I did the math.

I woke up tired and a hundred years older, and it was my turn to drive. Twelve hours straight and we got to Maryland near ten o'clock at night. I drove through my hometown like it was the first time I had ever been there. Arrow had fallen asleep with her forehead against the glass, and I turned the radio off and rolled my window down and let the night air flood the car. It was miraculously not muggy, and the air was thick with the smell of the ocean. I pulled into my driveway and turned off the engine. Grandma Doris was sitting in her rocking chair on the front porch. She raised a hand when she saw me. She was not wearing black.

I left Arrow in the car and went to hug Grandma. She wrapped her arms around me, and I felt the boniness of her arms like she was something too fragile to hold. Something too fragile to last. I don't know why I cried, but she smoothed down my hair and held me for a long time. When I finally pulled away, she was smiling.

"You look so much older," she whispered.

"I don't ever want you to die, okay?"

"Okay," she said. "But I think instead of hoping for the impossible, we should probably be thankful for the time we have now. And live every moment like it might be the last moment we have together."

"Wow, Grandma."

"Sitting shiva has done wonders for my outlook, Frances. I highly recommend the practice."

"Okay. I guess when you die, I'll sit shiva."

"Oh no. Don't be silly. I'm never going to die."

She hugged me again and then went to wake up Arrow. I took her place in the rocking chair and tried to feel thankful for the time I had now.

After a minute my phone rang. I took it upstairs and talked to Louis until I fell asleep.

The next morning my grandfather woke me up by sitting on the side of my bed heavily, collapsing onto the mattress with a small sigh. I squinted my eyes and tried to focus on him.

"Grandpa, it's really early," I said.

"It's actually noon," he replied. "And I'm only waking you up because you have a gentleman caller, as it were."

"A gentleman what?"

"Frances, there is a man here to see you," my grand-mother said, bursting into the room.

"A what?" I asked, sitting up in bed. My heart was suddenly racing. I had just talked to Louis. Did he take the red-eye to come see me? That didn't make any sense. Did I even want that? I didn't know if I even wanted that.

"A *man*," my grandmother said. She looked strangely agitated.

"Why does she look like that?" I asked my grandpa.

"He landed in her rosebushes," he replied. He patted my leg and left the room before I could reply.

He landed in her rosebushes?

I got out of bed and dressed quickly, brushing my teeth and smoothing my hair into a ponytail. I had mascara underneath my eyes and I licked my fingers and dragged them across my skin.

"So pretty," I whispered to my reflection. My reflection looked slightly terrified in response.

I went downstairs slowly because the front door was open and I could hear voices outside. I could hear a very specific voice outside. I could hear a very famous voice outside. Anybody in the country would be able to identify that voice.

I reached the front door and stepped onto the porch.

Oh.

He had landed in my grandmother's rosebushes.

That's where his helicopter was parked.

My grandmother was yelling at Wallace Green and his helicopter pilot while also managing to look sort of smitten with the idea of having Wallace Green and his helicopter on her front lawn. She kept looking up and down the street like she was checking to see if any neighbors were watching.

Wallace Green saw me and waved his hand hesitantly, and then he leaned toward my grandma and whispered to her. She stopped yelling and started smiling. She shrugged and laughed and went back into the house, brushing past me.

I walked up to Wallace Green and said, "You didn't fly that all the way from Austin, did you?"

"Well, no. I rented it in DC. I took a private jet and then my pilot convinced me to rent a helicopter instead of a car only because I think he likes being in the air more than he likes being on the ground," Wallace Green said.

"Oh, of course Wallace Green has a private jet," I said.

"He also has a private pilot," Wallace Green added.

"He also speaks in the third person, apparently."

"He does not, actually." Wallace Green stuck his hand

out to me. "I'm Anthony Green."

I looked at his hand but didn't shake it. "I'm sorry?"

"I'm Anthony. Anthony Green. Wallace is my brother," he explained.

He took his wallet out of his back pocket, fished out his license, and handed it to me. It said *Anthony Green* and it listed his birthday as December twenty-fifth (everybody knew Wallace Green's birthday was on Christmas, that's the only reason I checked).

"You're Wallace Green's brother?"

"Yes."

"Twin brother?"

"Identical twins, yes. It's nice to meet you."

He held out his hand again, and I shook it only because I wanted him to stop holding out his hand and that seemed like the fastest way to get that to happen.

"Oh God," I said, because I suddenly knew where this was going and I wasn't ready for it. I had driven to Austin and prepared myself for it the whole way and then I had driven home and unprepared myself for it and now I was here and everything was going wrong. This was wrong.

"I take it you're catching up," he said, his mouth an unreadable straight line.

He rubbed at his chin, and that's when I saw the bracelet on his wrist. It was big and silver and fitted with a thick chunk of turquoise.

I sat down on the grass, cross-legged, and he sat across

from me, keeping almost exactly one foot of space between us. I felt sick to my stomach, like something was going wrong inside my body, but at the same time there was a quiet refrain that played through my head to the beat of my heart, an unsteady rhythm that pulsed and grew inside me, and all it said was *she wasn't crazy, she wasn't crazy, she wasn't crazy* over and over until it stopped and I realized he had said something.

"What?" I asked.

"I said—I have so much to apologize for. I went through a very dark time in my life, and I made many, many terrible decisions."

It was remarkable how much he looked like Wallace Green. I didn't think I'd ever actually met identical twins before. There was something in me that didn't want to believe it, that tried to pretend this was really Wallace Green disguised as—well, as himself—but I knew that wasn't the truth. There were subtle, minute differences. Anthony Green looked smaller, somehow, either skinnier or a half inch shorter, I couldn't tell. And he looked like his natural resting face was apologetic, like he'd found a lot to be sorry for in the course of his life.

"I promise, Frances . . . I swear I didn't know about you," he continued. "I promise I didn't or else I would have . . ." He trailed off and looked out over the lawn, past our house to where the Miles River divided Easton from its other half.

"I know," I said. "She told me she never told you. Or, I guess, she told me she never told *him*. Sorry. This is all a little . . ."

This was so many things. I couldn't choose just one. Bizarre. Ridiculous. Unbelievable.

"I can't apologize enough. I was such a . . ." He paused again, laughed. I felt almost sorry for him but then, you know, didn't. "A lying asshole," he finished. "I did such terrible things back then, and I never imagined I would still be living with the consequences."

"You're calling me a consequence?" I whispered.

"No, that's not what I meant!"

"Look, I don't want a father figure. That's not why I went to Austin. My mom just died, okay, and she wanted me to find him. You. Him. Whatever."

"Wallace told me your mother passed away, and I am so sorry for your loss."

Behind him, Anthony Green's pilot was reading a magazine in their rented helicopter. It was actually kind of funny, funny enough that I had to fight the urge to laugh. I guess maybe that's how I knew I was going to be okay. Because I still felt like laughing, even though my real father was a liar who'd impersonated his twin brother in order to get my mother to sleep with him.

"Were there others?" I asked suddenly.

He didn't have to answer me. He just shook his head and said, "I'm so sorry. And I want to do everything I can to make it up to you. I wish I'd met you sooner, Frances. I wish I'd done so many things differently."

"I think I need a minute," I said.

"Sure."

"Could you just stay here, please?"

"Are you going somewhere?"

"I'll come back. Just stay there. Okay?"

"Okay, sure. Sure, I'll stay here."

I stood up and walked next door to Arrow's back door. Aunt Florence was chopping vegetables in the kitchen. When she saw me she said, "Oh, Frannie! I've missed your face around here. Arrow's still sleeping, but you can go ahead upstairs, of course."

"Thanks," I said, trying my best not to look like everything was crumpling inside me. I walked up the stairs and opened the door to Arrow's room. She was sleeping on her stomach with one leg off the bed, like a cartoon. I crawled in next to her.

"It's too early," she mumbled.

"Arrow," I whispered.

"Frannie? What are you doing here?"

"I have something to tell you."

Arrow opened her eyes properly and rolled over to face me. "What?" she asked.

"My mom's not a liar. My father is," I said. I could feel the smile spreading across my face.

I started laughing and then I started crying and then Arrow started crying, and I left my father waiting for a really long time but when I finally went back, he was still there.

EPILOGUE
Louis

I woke up the next morning to a series of buzzes from my phone. I'd forgotten to put it on silent the night before. It took a while for my brain to translate what the noise meant. I was still tired from driving so much in the span of a day and from spending one perfect night with Frannie in Austin and so I kept my eyes closed as I reached for the phone. When I finally peeked at the screen, I saw a long series of text messages from Frannie. I opened them up and read them twice before I understood what they meant.

And then I read the last two over again because they were:

I miss you, Louis.
You're one of the best things to ever come
out of the internet.

I set the phone back on the nightstand and I got up and took a shower and kept thinking about what I could say back, but everything I thought of seemed inappropriate or weird.

After I showered I got dressed and checked my phone again. I had a message from my mom, the following intricate string of emojis: a man, an airplane, four watches with different times on them, a palm tree, a taxi, a man and woman holding hands, a man and woman kissing, an arrow pointing to the left, a boy, a question mark.

Translation: *Dad is back! We're at the store. Come say hi.*

I went to wake Willa, but her bed was already empty and made. It might have been the first time in our lives I'd slept later than her. I got my phone and put my shoes on and went downstairs to my car.

I was starving and I couldn't remember the last time I'd gone this long without visiting Sally's Diner, so I pulled into the parking lot and turned the car off. Sally's was busy and nobody was at the host's stand so I waited by the door until Benson appeared from the kitchen. He face was red and he seemed flustered. When he saw me, he froze comically, one foot in front of the other and raised off the floor, his eyes wide. But then he remembered himself and started walking again. He raised his hand toward me. I couldn't remember ever shaking hands with Benson before, but I humored him. Something weird was going on. I was sure it had to do with my sister, and I was sure I didn't need to know what it was.

"You want something to eat?" he asked. "I'll get you something to eat. The usual? I'll get you the usual."

"And a coffee," I called as he disappeared into the kitchen again, but I didn't think he heard me.

I waited in a plastic chair by the door. He came out later with a white bag of food and a paper coffee cup. When I tried to pay him, he waved me off distractedly.

"Later, later," he said. "Next time, okay? Get me next time."

I found Willa sitting in the passenger seat of my car.

"How did you get here?" I asked her.

"I walked, dummy. I didn't get these expensive things for nothing. Did you get me something to eat? Are you going to the store? Give me a ride, okay?" She dug her hand into the bag and emerged with a fistful of tater tots.

"You wouldn't know why Benson is acting so weird, do you?" I asked, turning on the car and trying to salvage as many tater tots as I could before Willa ate them all.

"Nope," she said, drinking half my coffee in one sip, despite it being steaming hot. "Are you on your way to tell Mom and Dad you're moving to Austin? Because they're going to have heart attacks and die, you know? We're supposed to co-own this store and be weird shut-ins and never leave Los Angeles. They're not going to take this well."

"Yes, I'm on my way to the store to tell them. Please don't drink all my coffee. They're going to be fine. It will go fine."

She pulled a breakfast sandwich out of the bag and pulled it apart messily, handing me the smaller half.

"I would have just gotten you something," I said.

"This is more fun. Let's split lunch too."

I was still hungry when we got to the store, and I was also more nervous than I thought I would be. Willa opened the passenger door, and I told her to go in without me.

"Are you coming in?" she asked.

"I'll be there in a minute. I just need to sit here."

"Are you okay, Louis?"

"I'm going to go back to therapy," I told her.

She nodded solemnly and said, "You know I was kidding, right? When I told you that you didn't have your own tragedy. That was a shitty thing to say. Everyone has their own tragedies, you know? I'm glad you're trying to get a handle on yours."

"Thanks. I'm trying."

"Do you miss her?"

"This doesn't have anything to do with her."

"That's not what I said."

"Of course I miss her."

"I think she was really good for you," Willa said.

She got out of the car and left the food bag on the passenger seat.

It didn't escape me that she'd said *was*—Frannie *was* really good for me. Like I would never see her again.

I guess maybe I knew I would never see her again.

I reached into the bag. Willa had left me a few tater tots, and I ate them slowly, hardly tasting them, not paying attention.

Willa was exaggerating. My parents would be surprised by the news, but I knew they would understand that this made the most sense for me. They would understand that from the second the University of Texas had offered it to me, I'd already accepted the scholarship in my mind. I'd already committed. It was maybe the only thing I'd ever committed to.

I reached into the bag for another tater tot but felt something sharp instead. I grabbed the bag and looked inside but wasn't immediately sure of what I was looking at. I took the object out and turned it over. It was small and metal and sharp, and it left an inky stain on my fingers. And then of course I knew what it was.

And maybe one day I would drop it in the mail, but I thought I'd keep it for a little while first. It had found me, and maybe the things we found were the things we really needed, and the things we lost were the things we were never meant to have at all.

I put the nib into my pocket and went inside to talk to my parents.

I closed my TILT account that night. I would call Dr. Williams in the morning.

I texted Frannie.

> **It feels like everything has been turned on its head.**

She sent me back a heart-shaped emoji.

I'd never felt happier to let something go.

But it wasn't her. I wasn't letting her go.

I held on to her.

Acknowledgments

There is nothing quite like writing a book to make you realize how many supportive, encouraging humans surround you. To my little group: I am truly indebted to you and I couldn't be happier to have you in my weird little life, helping me write weird little stories like this one.

First, duh: my parents. Without you this book would not have been finished, period. I can't thank you enough so I'm not even going to try. And to the rest of my family, and especially my brothers, sisters-in-law, and my unimaginably perfect nieces. And Saige: who is old enough to read these acknowledgments but NOT old enough to read this book yet. Hi, Saige.

My agent, Wendy Schmalz, for believing in this book so much, for believing in me so much, for being a constant source of fresh air and good advice. You're the freaking coolest and I am thankful for you DAILY.

My small, lovely publishing family at HarperCollins and HarperTeen: starting with, of course, Jocelyn Davies, for loving this book and making it miles better. And to Michelle Taormina, Alison Donalty, Alexei Esikoff, Elizabeth Ward, Stephanie Hoover and Margot Wood and the Epic Reads crew, for all being part of the village that wrangled these sentences into a real live book.

Kim Nguyen, for letting me ask you four hundred questions about Vietnamese culture, and for letting Arrow borrow your necklace (without even asking!). Zach Weaver, for knowing so much about tennis. Seriously, so much. It's almost weird. Megan Weaver, for graphic designing my internet persona into someone who looks much more professional than I actually am. Evan Lesner, for talking to your rabbi about shiva and for knowing the streets of downtown Los Angeles like the back of your hand. Tim Laramy, for having a house on the Miles River and letting me stay there. Mary Clark, for horse knowledge. Matt Gallivan, for unparalleled Facebook wrangling skills. Darlena Cunha, for championing so hard for my first book and for writing really cool internet stuff. Aaron Karo and Georgina Bruce, for being constant sounding boards and sources of calm whenever I threatened to give up writing (which is, what, twice a week?). Ken MacLeod, for support and encouragement from very far away.

Shane, the first person who knew who Frannie's father really was, and who told me, at the very beginning: "This sounds OK, but I think you can do better." Thanks for always making me do better.

Still: Sarah Dotts Barley. The best.

Last (but very much not least):

All the freaking sweet, beautiful souls who've tweeted or emailed or commented or faved or reposted or done various other stuff you can do on social media and the like. I appreciate every single message and every single moment you took to write to me.

JOIN THE

Epic Reads
COMMUNITY

THE ULTIMATE YA DESTINATION

◀ **DISCOVER** ▶
your next favorite read

◀ **MEET** ▶
new authors to love

◀ **WIN** ▶
free books

◀ **SHARE** ▶
infographics, playlists, quizzes, and more

◀ **WATCH** ▶
the latest videos

◀ **TUNE IN** ▶
to Tea Time with Team Epic Reads